Chemung County

An Illustrated History

Produced in cooperation with
the Chemung County Historical Society
and the Chemung County Chamber of Commerce

Table of Contents

Chemung County

~∞∞∞∞~

An Illustrated History

Produced in cooperation with
The Chemung County Historical Society
415 E. Water Street
Elmira, New York 14901
and
The Chemung County Chamber of Commerce
400 East Church Street
Elmira, New York 14901

Text by Amy H. Wilson
Corporate Profiles by Peg Gallagher

Community Communications, Inc.
Publishers: Ronald P. Beers and
James E. Turner
Publisher's Sales Associate: Bonnie Brutsman
Acquisitions: William McAllister
Executive Editor: James E. Turner
Senior Editor: Mary Shaw Hughes
Managing Editor: Bonnie Ashley Harris
Editorial Assistant: Amanda Joy Burbank
Contract Manager: Christi Stevens
Profile Editors: Kari Collin Jarnot and
Mary Catherine Richardson
Design Director: Scott Phillips
Designer: Matt Johnson
Photo Editor: Amy H. Wilson
Production Manager: Jarrod Stiff
Sales Assistant: Annette Lozier
Proofreader: Amanda Joy Burbank
Accounting Services: Sara Ann Turner
Printing Production: Gary G. Pulliam/DC Graphics
Pre-Press and Separations: Artcraft Graphic Productions

C C I

Community Communications, Inc.
Montgomery, Alabama
James E. Turner, *Chairman of the Board*
Ronald P. Beers, *President*
Daniel S. Chambliss, *Vice President*

(Title Page) Iroquois trade silver.
Photo by Milo Stewart Jr.

Foreword

The Chemung County Historical Society and Chemung County Chamber of Commerce are pleased to present for your reading enjoyment this new volume on the history of the Chemung Valley area. Within the scope of the Chemung County Historical Society's mission, we are charged with the activity to present publications that are "relevant to and consistent with the purposes and activities of the Society." With this most recent volume, *Chemung County, An Illustrated History*, our team of writers, museum curator Amy H. Wilson and retired journalist Peg Gallagher, have crafted a text that serves to present historical information of our county and its region up to the close of the 20th century. Royalties from the sale of this volume go to the Society and Chamber as sponsoring organizations.

The writers of our regional history here in the Southern Tier of New York state who came before us, left a legacy of text—Ausburn Towner, Charles Barber, Clark Wilcox, Thomas Byrne, Harry B. Kelsey, G. Welles and George Crandall, Alfred Hilbert, J. Arthur Kieffer, Eva Taylor, and many more. Countless authors have also contributed to the historical society's quarterly journal, adding their voices to those who cared enough to record history's moments.

Ausburn Towner's history of the county, published in 1892, included in its title the phrase ". . . from the closing of the 18th century," adding 19th century information to our record of history. In 1976, the historical society published Tom Byrne's history of Chemung County with an introductory phrase ". . . 'bringing Towner up-to-date." Most recently in 1998, our volume *Images of America: The Chemung Valley* by Diane L. Janowski and Allen C. Smith, provides an fascinating pictorial history of our community. Today, in the penultimate year of the 20th century, we are pleased to offer this volume that continues the legacy of recording the "history of our county and its people."

As you read this volume, be aware of the legacy that precedes it, a legacy of writers that have recorded the stories and events of this Chemung Valley region for the enjoyment and knowledge of future generations. The continuous flow of the historical record is an important and constant reminder to all of us of where we have come from and how we can chart our course for the future.

The history volume you are holding offers a concluding statement about the people of the Chemung Valley ". . . they are filled with possibilities and new hope as they stand on the threshold of the new millennium." Historians and writers tell of what has come in the centuries before us. It is now up to us to act and then record that history for the next century for those who will come after us. ✑

Constance B. Barone
Director
Chemung County Historical Society

Preface

For more than two centuries, the natural beauty of Chemung County has attracted residents and visitors alike. In 1889, the young writer, Rudyard Kipling, visited Chemung County in search of one of his heroes, Mark Twain, who spent summers in Elmira from 1870 to 1903. Kipling remarked on the "pleasant, fat, little hills" that surround Chemung Valley, and when he reached Twain's hilltop homestead, he concluded it to be an ideal place for writing. In Elmira, Twain found an environment that stimulated his creativity. He wrote eloquently of his octagonal study on East Hill and its views of the "retreating ranges of distant blue hills." It is this beauty that has sustained the people in Chemung County through celebrations and heartaches.

This book is not meant to be a comprehensive history of Chemung County. Instead, it is a concise story focusing on the economic history of the area. The scope of the project does not allow me to do justice to important topics like education, religion, and government. In this volume I have tried to address a few myths and bring new scholarship to some popular topics in local history.

There are many people (and organizations) who have contributed to this book by commenting on early drafts, providing source material, or identifying and contributing illustrations. For their generous help, I would like to thank the following: Constance B. Barone/Chemung County Historical Society; Elizabeth B. Monroe; Bonnie Stacy/Tioga Point Museum; George Hamell/New York State Museum; Craig Williams/New York State Museum; James Folts/New York State Archives; Joseph Meany/New York State Museum; Robert Mulligan; Carolyn Brady; Hency Yuen-Eng; Kevin Keeley/Chemung County Chamber of Commerce; Mark Woodhouse/Mark Twain Archives, Elmira College; Howard Broock; Tom Byrne; Michael Horigan; Dolores Elliott; George Farr; Wendy Chmielewsky/Swarthmore College Peace Collection; Milo Stewart, Jr./Hartwick College; Michael Gramly; Gretchen Sharlow/Center for Mark Twain Studies; Mark Twain House; and Janet Newcomb/The Arts of the Southern Finger Lakes. ৳

Amy H. Wilson

Chapter 1

EARLY INHABITANTS

*Throughout the history of
Chemung County, the
Chemung River has determined
routes of travel for the Native
Americans and later the settlers,
at times inspiring them to settle
near its banks and at other
times providing a pathway to
different territories. Courtesy of
Chemung County Historical
Society, Inc.*

*L*ocated at the southern edge of the Finger Lakes region of Upstate New York, Chemung County has always been known for its natural beauty. The Chemung River, for which the county is named, begins at the Tioga River near Painted Post and flows east through the county to meet the Susquehanna River in Pennsylvania. At the center of the county, the flat river valley extends to a width of about four miles. Here lies the county seat of Elmira along with other towns and villages. Chemung County is centrally located in New York's Southern Tier and borders Pennsylvania to the south. The beauty of the landscape and its proximity to the Finger Lakes have made the Chemung Valley a magnet for visitors over the last few centuries.

The scenic hills surrounding the Chemung Valley were shaped more than 12,000 years ago when glacial ice moved as far south as Pennsylvania. This process created the body of water we now know as the Chemung River and pushed it towards the Susquehanna River at Athens, Pennsylvania. The ice sheet destroyed vegetation and animal life until a warming trend created an arctic tundra landscape. The semi-arctic conditions attracted prehistoric animals like the caribou, giant beaver, mastodon, and wooly mammoth that fed on the grasses and shrubs near streams and marshy areas and unwittingly gave us the name of our river and county. Thousands of years after these creatures walked the region, Native Americans discovered a large horn (or tusk) along the river (most likely that of a mastodon) and called the area *Chemung*, or "Place of the Horn."

The Chemung River determined routes of travel for the Native Americans, at times inspiring them to settle near its banks and at other times providing a pathway to different territories. The area is best known as the territory of the Senecas and Cayugas, part of the Five Nations of the Iroquois Confederacy. But these tribes did not control the region until the 17th century. As far back as 10,000 BC, the Chemung Valley had been home to several other native populations. After the glacial ice had retreated and the climate warmed enough to support human habitation, people known as Paleo Indians settled across the Southern Tier from Steuben County to Oneonta and beyond. Archaeologists discovered evidence of these people north of Corning at Lamoka Lake. Most likely, the Paleo Indians moved camp seasonally in search of food sources and lived here for about 1,000 years until, perhaps, a colder climate eventually drove them south.

After 900 AD, a warming trend, among other factors, attracted new inhabitants who lived in villages and practiced horticulture based on corn, beans, and squash. These people may have been the ancestors of the Iroquoian speaking people who later dominated the area. In the 15th century, the

Chemung or "Place of the Horn" was the name given to the area by the Native Americans after discovering a large horn or tusk—most likely that of a woolly mammoth (pictured here) or a mastadon. Courtesy of New York State Museum.

Southern Tier of New York and Northern Tier of Pennsylvania were home to Iroquoians whose descendents would later be known as the Susquehannocks or Andastes. These were Iroquoian people who never joined the Iroquois Confederacy. They abandoned this area in the late 16th century and moved south toward Lancaster County, Pennsylvania, leaving the Chemung Valley without permanent settlements until well into the 17th century.

The Senecas were an Iroquoian speaking people who occupied the western part of New York beginning just north of Chemung County. By the 16th century, the Iroquois were involved in constant warfare among themselves and their neighbors. To provide greater security, villages started joining together to create larger communities. In this climate of war developed a confederacy called the League of the Iroquois. By 1525, five nations of Iroquois people (Mohawks, Oneidas, Onondagas, Cayugas, and Senecas) had come together in what amounted to a mutual non-aggression pact. This later developed into a federated form of "government." Their homelands stretched across central New York like a longhouse, and as the westernmost group, the Senecas were called the "Keepers of the Western Door." Every action by this new confederacy required unanimous decision, the concept of majority rule was not accepted. The confederacy allowed the individual nations to follow their own policies as long as their actions did not harm another member of the League. The biggest weakness of the confederation was that the system did not allow for quick authoritarian decisions. This would later become the League's downfall during the American Revolution.

By the 18th century the Seneca lands stretched south to include the Chemung Valley, while the Cayuga lands reached the lower portion of the valley near Tioga Point. The Senecas had become the most populous of the Five Nations and had the most influ-

Chemung County archaeologist A. Frank Barrott at the Lamoka Lake site north of Corning, New York. Courtesy of Chemung County Historical Society, Inc.

ence in the area. They suffered the same losses from war and disease as the other Iroquois nations but they were more aggressive in replacing their population. From 1670 to 1730, the Seneca population dropped from 4,000 to 1,400, but by the time of the American Revolution their numbers were back to 4,000. They achieved this by assimilating *adoptees* captured during wars with other tribes like the Huron, Illinois, and Andaste. When Europeans first encountered the Seneca villages, they found a system of longhouses that were home to three or more families. The longhouse consisted of several hearth units attached to each other end-to-end housing matrilineal family units. Later, as conflict and assimilation continued to ravage the social structure by breaking down blood lineages, the Senecas lived in one- and two-family cabins similar to those used by the white settlers.

Lamoka points and a netsinker found in the Chemung Valley Region. Courtesy of Chemung County Historical Society, Inc.

There has always been dispute over who were the first Europeans to visit the Chemung Valley. One popular 19th-century theory claimed that French explorer Etienne Brulé, a scout for Samuel de Champlain, deserved this distinction. In 1615, Champlain sent him on a mission from Niagara to find Andaste allies for an attack on the Iroquois. Brulé journeyed south from Niagara to the Susquehanna. Although Brulé's route is uncertain, the easiest course would have been via the Chemung River, therefore, 19th-century historians surmised that he passed through our valley.

Brulé brought back tales of having found a large fortified settlement which later historians placed on Spanish Hill along the east bank of the Chemung, just below Waverly, New York. But current scholarship and archaeological evidence indicate there was no such settlement in that area in 1615 and that Brulé might have invented some of his accounts to cover for his failure to rendezvous with Champlain at the appointed date. Champlain included details of Brulé's expedition in his 1618 *Voyages*, yet he omitted the story in subsequent editions of the book.

The possibility exists that white traders came to this region prior to the late 18th century, though this is unproven. Documented sources indicate the area remained free of Europeans until the 1760s, when Moravians, using pathways already established by the Native Americans, traveled through on their way to Ohio. But the Senecas were guardians of what 20th-century writers have called the Forbidden Trail, connecting all of the major Indian villages from Tioga Point on the Susquehanna River through the Chemung Valley to the Allegheny River and westward to Ohio. Although forbidden to whites and to Indian enemies, the path was probably the easiest route to the western territories from the centers of colonial population. Unauthorized users of the trail, if caught, were subjected to punishment. The first European to successfully navigate the trail was a Moravian missionary who traveled with Native American Christian converts in 1767.

In the mid-18th century there were several Indian villages established along the Chemung River. These were not only Seneca, but also included Delaware and Cayuga among others. At the eastern end of what would become the county was the village of New Chemung. Moving west there was

Tioga Point, the confluence of the Chemung and Susquehanna Rivers. Courtesy of the Tioga Point Museum, Tioga, PA.

Rich farmland lies along the Chemung River in the Chemung Valley. This is a late nineteenth century view looking northwest toward Elmira from the site of the Battle of Newtown (1779). Courtesy of Chemung County Historical Society, Inc.

Newtown (near present day Lowman), Middletown, three villages around present day Elmira, Runonvea (Big Flats), and Assinisink (Corning). By the 1750s, the traditional longhouse was used only as a public meeting place and a rest stop for visitors. Seneca life in the Chemung Valley mostly was spent growing huge fields of corn, beans, and squash (especially pumpkins); and traveling to white settlements to trade furs and other goods.

Between 1689 and 1760, there was fighting among the British and French. The Iroquois generally had hoped to remain neutral in these disagreements because they served as middlemen in trade between the two nations' colonies. The western Senecas traditionally sided with the French, but more eastern tribes sided with the British. Both sides needed extra manpower, and each tried to persuade the Iroquois to become allies. But in 1763, after the French defeat in the Seven Years War, the Treaty of Paris removed the French as a threat to British interests in the new world. With this development, the Iroquois realized that the British colonies no longer needed them as allies. The British also now had the ability to travel to formerly French territory to buy furs directly, thus eliminating the Iroquois middleman. The natives certainly had cause to fear for their security. When tensions started to rise between the British and their colonists, the League hoped they would be able to remain neutral in the conflict. Unfortunately their neutrality would not last. ◄§

Chapter 2

NEWTOWN TO ELMIRA

*Cabin of Chemung County's
first settler, John Hendy, located
on present day Rorick's Glen
Parkway. Courtesy of Chemung
County Historical Society, Inc.*

In 1775, when war began between American colonists and the British, the Iroquois Confederacy along with the Senecas' lifestyle in the Chemung Valley was on the verge of breaking apart. Although some in the Confederacy were pro-American, others, like the Senecas, were generally pro-British. The Iroquois chiefs met to find a consensus but in 1777, as the first fighting began in upstate New York, they gave up the attempt. Attacks by American revolutionaries and strong persuasion by pro-British colonists soon convinced most Iroquois to side with the British. In 1778, many Native Americans joined the British and Loyalist troops in attacks on frontier settlements like Wyoming, Pennsylvania, and Cherry Valley, New York. These actions caused the settlers to demand protection from the Continental Army.

In the winter of 1778-1779, General George Washington drew up the plans for a campaign through northern Pennsylvania and New York against the Iroquois and appointed General John Sullivan its commander. Sullivan gathered three brigades at Wilkes-Barre, Pennsylvania and traveled north along the Susquehanna River. General James Clinton, commanding the New York brigade, was directed to march southward from the Mohawk Valley to join Sullivan's troops at the confluence of the Chemung and Susquehanna Rivers. The army had two goals: to destroy the food supply to the Iroquois and British troops, which the Seneca provided from their own bountiful crops; and to permanently remove the Native Americans from the conflict. The expedition got underway in the summer of 1779, and Sullivan and Clinton joined forces by the end of August.

Iroquois chief Joseph Brant led raids as far as southeastern New York in an attempt to divert the campaign but with little success. Sullivan's and Clinton's combined forces marched through Cayuga and Seneca territory, facing serious fighting only near the village of Newtown on the Chemung River on August 29th. In about seven hours from the first shots of the battle, Sullivan's troops managed to take control of the village by forcing British troops and Iroquois into retreat. Within the next two days, almost all of the Native American's crops and villages in the Chemung Valley had been destroyed by the Continental Army.

The immediate effect of the campaign was to cause the Iroquois to retreat to Fort Niagara and seek refuge with the British. Sullivan, however, failed to achieve the long-term objective of permanently removing the Iroquois from the war. In fact, the effects of the campaign were to increase the Iroquois' hostility, resulting in more raiding activity along the frontier; and to make them more dependent on British resources. The Treaty of Paris (1783), which ended the Revolutionary War, forced the British to cede all lands south of Canada and east of the Mississippi River to the United States. This area included lands the British had originally reserved for the Iroquois in the 1768 Treaty of Fort Stanwix. The New York legislature opened up this new western territory to white expansion by distributing tracts of land as payment to soldiers in the Continental Army. The Sullivan-Clinton Campaign indirectly facilitated white settlement of the Chemung Valley. The soldiers who fought in Sullivan's army were struck by the beauty of the region and returned home with glowing reports of this fertile valley. In 1784, the first white permanent settlement began here.

Although few veterans of Sullivan's campaign settled here, the white men who brought their families to this area had fought at the battles of Bunker Hill and Saratoga. They built log cabins and frame houses, gristmills and taverns and went about the business of making new lives for themselves. Many of the early settlers came up the Susquehanna River from Wilkes-Barre, Pennsylvania or moved west from Connecticut. Senecas and other native

In the winter of 1778-1779, General John Sullivan was appointed commander by General George Washington of the campaign led through northern Pennsylvania and New York against the Iroquois. Artist, Lawrence E. Eyres. Courtesy of Chemung County Historical Society, Inc.

groups who had refused to abandon their land also lived in the Chemung Valley. As whites settled the area, the Seneca proceeded to collect taxes from them in the form of crop offerings.

Sources indicate the multiple ethnic groups lived peaceably together, but in 1790, white men in Pennsylvania murdered two Senecas, prompting a new treaty with the United States government. In 1791, President Washington appointed Colonel Timothy Pickering to act as agent for the government and assure the Iroquois of their security. The Seneca chief Red Jacket negotiated on behalf of the Indians. The original plan called for members of both parties to meet at Painted Post, located at the western end of the Chemung River, to negotiate a treaty. But negotiations were held at Newtown because Pickering's boats could not travel further up the river. He brought reparation offerings (in the form of supplies) to the Iroquois, and an agreement was signed in June 1791 that effectively ended warfare between the Iroquois and the United States. In 1797, with the Treaty of Big Tree (near Geneseo), the Seneca sold most of their land in western New York and accepted 310 square miles of reservation along the Genesee River. At least a few Seneca remained in the Chemung Valley as late as 1809.

Meanwhile the development of what is now Chemung County was well underway. In 1788, the New York legislature created the Township of Chemung as part of Montgomery County. The township covered the area of the present county and about

Iroquois Chief Joseph Brant.
Artist, Lawrence E. Eyres. Courtesy of
Chemung County Historical Society, Inc.

1,000 inhabitants scattered in settlements throughout the valley from Chemung to Big Flats. Chemung was the first village of any size, but people soon discovered a more accessible and strategic location for a settlement where Newtown Creek empties into the Chemung River. The new settlement (on the site of present day Elmira) was called Newtown. Henry Wisner, the landowner, laid out the roads of the village and then created a second, adjacent village called Wisnerburg.

In February 1791, part of Montgomery County, including Chemung Township, split to form the new Tioga County. Another landowner, Guy Maxwell, laid out a third village, DeWittsburg, between Newtown and Wisnerburg. In 1792, these three villages were officially joined to form the village of Newtown, and the state legislature created the Town of Newtown from within the borders of Chemung Township. The first town meeting was held in May of that year at William Dunn's tavern. A few years later, Newtown became the site of the first county courthouse, a two-story log and clapboard structure housing the sheriff, a jail, and a courtroom. By the end of the 18th century, Chemung Township included several other settlements: Big Flats (established in 1787), Southport (1788), Horseheads (1789), Van Etten (1795), and Veteran (1800). Baldwin and Erin followed in 1813 and 1817 respectively.

As the 19th century began, the frontier citizens of Chemung Township worked hard to forge community bonds. They labored on their farms; worked in saw mills, grist mills, and distilleries; set up shop in taverns and general stores; held church services in their homes; organized quilting bees; and raced their horses on Sundays. Other signs of community bonding included the organization of a Masonic lodge in 1793. Newspapers were also important to the early settlement period, helping to create a common sense of purpose among the citizens in the Chemung Valley. As early as 1815, Murphy and Prindle published their weekly

*A George Washington Peace Medal, 1793.
Courtesy of Chemung County Historical
Society, Inc.*

RED JACKET.

*Senaca Chief Red Jacket wearing the George Washington Peace Medal.
Courtesy of Chemung County Historical Society, Inc.*

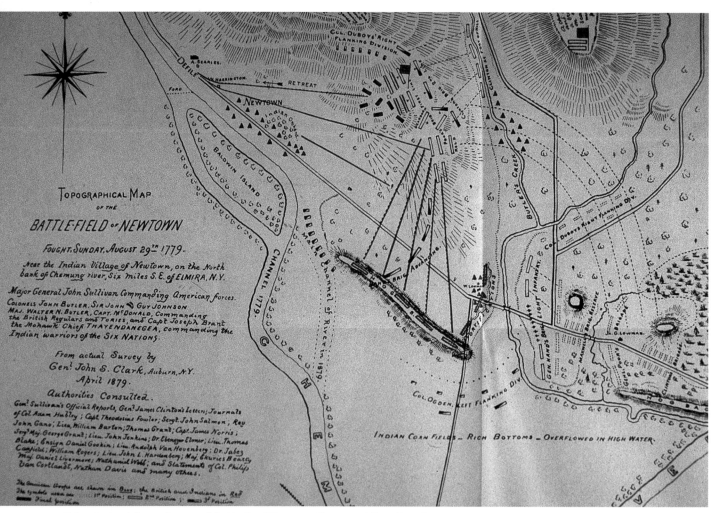

Print of a hand drawn diagram of the Battle of Newtown. Courtesy of Tioga Point Museum, Tioga, PA.

Telegraph in Newtown. By 1819, two additional weeklies, *The Vedette* and *The Investigator*, served as competition.

The citizens of the Town of Newtown began to build an infrastructure to better provide for themselves and to develop easier communication with the outside world. In 1803, the New York legislature authorized the construction of a turnpike from Newtown to Seneca Lake. The road, completed in 1807, was the beginning of what is now Lake Street in Elmira. A ferry crossed the Chemung River at Madison Avenue, but increased traffic demanded a bridge. In 1824, the Elmira and Southport Bridge

Company completed construction of a bridge at the intersection of Lake and Water Streets. In 1828, the legislature chartered the Tioga Coal, Iron, Mining, and Manufacturing Company with the charge of improving the navigation of the Chemung River through the construction of towpaths, dams, and locks.

In 1808, the Town of Newtown, the borders of which stretched from Pennsylvania to Seneca Lake, became Elmira, but the village kept its name until 1828, when it officially changed to Elmira as well. Although the origins of the name are disputed, the most frequently told version of the story takes place at Nathan Teall's tavern in

Newtown. Judge Emanuel Coryell came to the tavern to hold a meeting with his constituents. Discussion at the meeting focused on the desire to rename the town. Elmira Teall, the young daughter of the tavern owner, made her presence known by running in and out of the room while her mother repeatedly called her name aloud. Someone present then suggested the town should be named Elmira, and everyone agreed because they wanted a name that would set their town apart from the others. The century was still new and the citizens of Elmira were optimistic about their future.

The first courthouse in Chemung County. Courtesy of Chemung County Historical Society, Inc.

Original Sullivan's Monument at Newtown Battlefield, dedicated by General William T. Sherman in 1879. It was replaced with a new monument in 1912. Courtesy of Chemung County Historical Society, Inc.

Chapter 3

OPENING MARKETS

*The people pictured here were
members of prominent families
who helped settle the community
and founded many local businesses.
(L to R)
Mrs. Robert Covell,Jr.,
Stephen Covell, Edmund Covell,
Marianna Arnot Ogden, Mrs.
Strong, and Mrs. Arnot.*

The Chemung Canal opened in 1833 after much anticipation. This is a view of Lock 49 where the canal entered the Chemung River in downtown Elmira. Courtesy of Chemung County Historical Society, Inc.

The years between 1833 and the end of the Civil War brought considerable growth to Chemung County. Community leaders sought to expand the influence and position of the village of Elmira through construction of canals and railroads. Despite occasional setbacks, Elmira became a transportation hub.

The Chemung Canal opened in 1833 after much anticipation. The New York State Canal Commission began considering the route of the canal in the mid-1820s, but several years of public debate passed before any action. In 1829, the state legislature passed the Chemung Canal Bill, and construction began by the fall of 1830. The canal connected Seneca Lake, Millport, and Horseheads, then headed southeast toward Elmira, joining the Chemung River where Clemens Center Parkway is today.

The towns along the route of the canal prospered. Millvale changed its name to Millport when it became one of the centers of canal operation, and by 1855, it boasted more than 25 lock tenders. Horseheads, where the Chemung Canal intersected the canal extension to Corning, also benefited from canal traffic. After the canal opened, boat building became a large local industry in Millport and Elmira.

Construction was slow at first because of insufficient labor and poor design. Dishonest sub-contractors failed to pay many workers. Lack of state funding halted work between February 1831 and the summer of 1832, while changes in design drove up the cost of construction. But flooding, more than anything, delayed completion of the canal until October 1833.

The money-saving decision to build locks of wood instead of stone hampered the Chemung Canal throughout its existence. Wooden locks required continual maintenance, and state funds were inadequate for needed repairs. By 1840, only seven years after the canal opened, deterioration caused by increased traffic forced the state to rebuild

John Arnot, one of Chemung County's most prominent citizens and business leaders. Courtesy of
Chemung County Historical Society, Inc.

John W. Jones, an escaped slave who arrived in Elmira in 1844, was appointed sexton of the First Baptist Church in Elmira in 1847. He learned to read and write and assisted hundreds of fugitive slaves in finding their freedom. Courtesy of Chemung County Historical Society, Inc.

52 of the canal's 53 locks. Further rebuilding and repair work began in 1856.

Despite these troubles, the canal opened new markets, bringing great commercial success to the area. During a national depression in 1845, the Chemung Canal saw record traffic levels especially in Pennsylvania coal, the largest commodity transported on the canal. Western New York shipped gypsum, salt, and lime to distant markets. In 1846, Corning shipped $16 million worth of goods, including 87 million feet of lumber.

The final link between New York and Pennsylvania came with the construction of the Junction Canal in the 1850s, providing easier access to Pennsylvania's coal resources. The Junction Canal Company, backed by Elmira businessman John Arnot (one of Chemung County's most prominent citizens), began building this link between the Chemung Canal and Pennsylvania's North Branch Canal in March 1853 and completed it in 1856.

The Chemung Valley prospered largely because of its diverse manufacturing and commercial enterprises. Anticipating this economic growth, a group of investors, including John Arnot, organized the area's first bank in 1833. The Chemung Canal Bank was built at 415 East Water Street in Elmira and remained there until 1920.

Even with the success of the canals, the main mode of passenger transportation at this time was the horse-drawn stagecoach. Covering only 40 miles each day, the coaches and horses had to be strong to withstand the uneven roads filled with stumps and potholes. Passengers had to endure unheated coaches in the winter and hot, dusty travel in the summer. In 1847, a modern wood surfaced "plank road" eased traveling difficulties on the eight-mile stretch from Elmira to the Pennsylvania state line.

Railroads brought the greatest improvement in transportation for Chemung County. Chartered in 1832, the New York & Erie Railway, because of financial troubles, was

In July 1864, Camp Rathbun (located on a 30-acre-site between West Water Street and the Chemung River) became the site of a camp for Confederate prisoners. Courtesy of Chemung County Historical Society, Inc.

not completed between Binghamton (to the east) and Elmira until October 1849. The finished line connected the Chemung Valley to New York City and other major markets. To extend a railroad north of Chemung County, a group of businessmen, again led by John Arnot, financed construction of the Chemung Railroad (opened in December 1849) connecting Elmira to Watkins Glen. In 1851, the westward line of the New York & Erie Railroad became the longest continuous rail line in the world. To celebrate its completion, President Millard Fillmore and his cabinet traveled the new route and stopped in Elmira to give speeches and spend the night.

Between 1850 and 1855 Elmira's population doubled in part because the boundaries of the village expanded to incorporate land south of the Chemung River, and in part because of the labor force required to support the growing transportation network and resulting industries. Much of this labor was foreign born. Irish immigrants manned a majority of the locks on the Chemung Canal. German immigrants, largely from the Hesse-Darmstadt region, formed a significant part of the growing population of Chemung County from the 1840s through the 1860s. Previous to this period, most Germans in the Chemung Valley had migrated north from Pennsylvania.

In the 1840s, Elmira's African-American population increased by more than 350 percent, mostly due to escaped slaves seeking freedom. One escaped slave, John W. Jones, along with two step-brothers and two slaves from a nearby estate, escaped his owner in Leesburg, Virginia, in June 1844, arriving in Elmira the following month. He took odd jobs and, with the help of a tutor, learned to read and write. He was appointed sexton of the First Baptist Church in Elmira in 1847 and later purchased an adjacent house on Church Street.

In 1850, Congress passed the Fugitive Slave Law, which expanded federal powers to protect interests of slaveholders and required local government officials to return fugitive slaves to their owners. The law led many northerners to become anti-slavery sympathizers and greatly increased activity on the "Underground Railroad," a network of secret routes to freedom taken by fugitive slaves. No longer safe in northern states, large numbers of slaves fled to Canada. Because Elmira was on a north-south rail line that stretched all the way to Niagara Falls, the city was a regular stop on the Underground Railroad between Pennsylvania and the Canadian border.

As the local "station master," John W. Jones worked with William Still, his Underground counterpart in Philadelphia, to transport fugitive slaves into Canada. Jones regularly concealed parties of six to ten or more fugitives at a time in his home before he helped sneak them onto Northern Central Railroad baggage cars for their journey north. His efforts were aided financially by prominent local citizens such as Jervis Langdon and Rev. Thomas K. Beecher (brother of author Harriet Beecher Stowe). Jones's abolitionist friends claimed he helped nearly 800 slaves find their freedom during the 1850s.

When the Civil War began in 1861, converging rail lines and waterways made Elmira the logical choice for a military rendezvous point, one of three in New York State. Troops mustered at four barracks, including Camp Number Three ("Camp Rathbun") located on a 30-acre site between West Water Street and the Chemung River, with Hoffman Street being its eastern boundary. The city bustled with wartime activity brought on by the presence of military warehouses, two military hospitals, artillery ranges, and military police barracks. More than 20,000 officers and enlisted men from Chemung County and the surrounding region were sent south to the frontline from Elmira.

Union guards' quarters at the confederate prison camp. The structure in the foreground was one of two observation towers where local citizens paid 15 cents for a 15 minute glimpse of the prisoners across the street. *Courtesy of Chemung County Historical Society, Inc.*

In July 1864, Camp Rathbun became the site of a camp for Confederate prisoners who were transferred by train from an overcrowded prison in Maryland. Army officials had requested that the camp house between 8,000 and 10,000 men, but in reality it was only equipped for 5,000. One week after opening, a medical inspector found a shortage of blankets, insufficient food, inadequate care for the sick, and a pond ready to spread disease. By the end of August, the prison's population reached 9,500, while prisoners died at a rate of eight per day. The prison camp officially closed in July 1865, having housed more than 12,000 prisoners overall. During the year the camp was open, 2,963 men died, making Elmira's death rate double the average of all other Union camps.

After the prison camp was established, a half-acre in Woodlawn Cemetery was set aside to bury the dead Confederate soldiers. John W. Jones, who had become sexton for the cemetery, arrived every day at the gates of the prison to collect the dead and transport them for burial. The military paid him two dollars and fifty cents per burial. In all, Jones filled two acres with Confederate graves and amassed enough money to purchase some farmland near the cemetery following the war. The federal government declared Woodlawn a national cemetery in 1874.

By the end of the Civil War, Chemung County had experienced tremendous growth in population and industry, spurred by the introduction of canals and railroads. Elmira's population had increased significantly, and in 1864, the village was incorporated as a city. The next 50 years would prove to be the biggest era of growth for the county. ❧

Confederate graves at Woodlawn National Cemetery. In 1907, these gravestones replaced the original wooden markers erected by John W. Jones. Courtesy of Chemung County Historical Society, Inc.

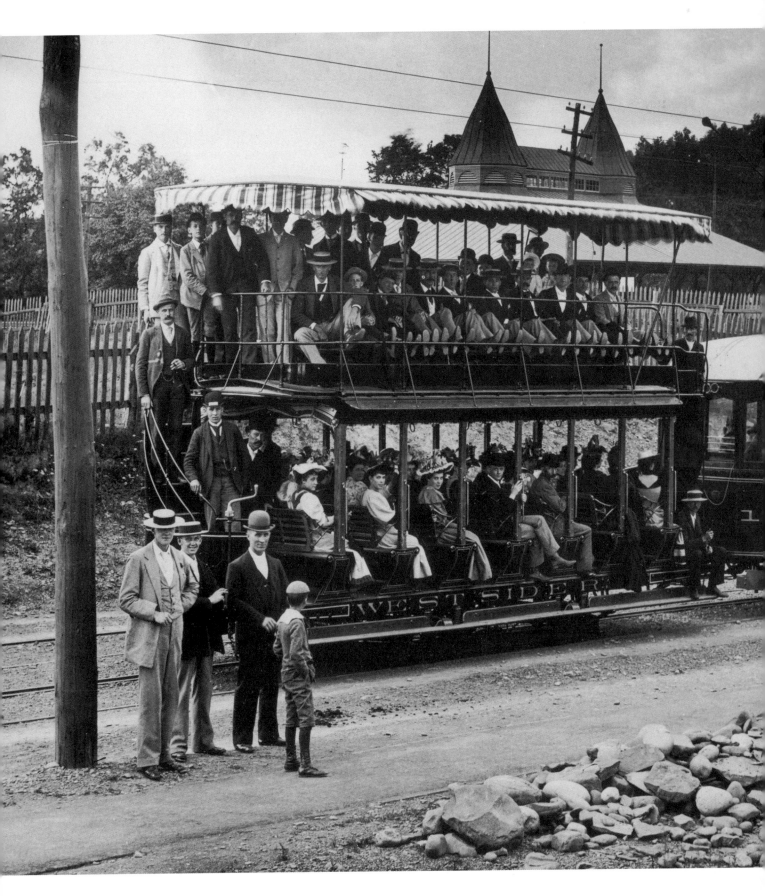

Chapter 4

THE YEARS OF EXPANSION

This crowded trolley car is in route to Eldridge Park, one of the first landscaped parks in the Chemung Valley. Courtesy of Chemung County Historical Society, Inc.

The period following the Civil War through the early part of the 20th century was one of unprecedented economic and population growth for Chemung County. Elmira was incorporated as a city in 1864 and elected its first mayor. In 1865, the population in Elmira was about 12,000. By 1890, the population had grown by more than 157 percent to reach 30,893. The city flourished from 1880 through 1930, as the population rose steadily. Chemung County courted new industry by setting aside the area of what is now Elmira Heights as an industrial community.

The village of Elmira Heights began as a private corporation in 1892. Matthias Arnot, of Chemung Canal Bank; Spencer Mead, of the Northern Central Railroad; and Charles Langdon, along with other local businessmen, formed the Elmira Industrial Association with the intention of luring industries to the Elmira area. With $100,000 in capital they purchased almost 500 acres of prime land north of the city and divided it into large factory sites along the rail lines with smaller sites fronting the streets. In October 1892, the corporation established a property lottery where nearly 2,000 investors bought the right to an unspecified lot, the location of which was determined during a one-day lottery in October 1893.

By 1895, at least nine factories operated in the new community, including Elmira Knitting Mills, Elmira Bridge Works, and Eclipse Bicycle Company. The addition of homes, schools, and stores made the area a neighborhood. To attract more people to the new community, the corporation built the Oak Ridge Hotel complete with an outdoor dance pavilion and offered entertainment such as cock fighting and wrestling. The corporation also built the Conewawah Inn as a

Elmira Knitting Mills was one of at least nine factories operating in Elmira Heights in 1895. Courtesy of Chemung County Historical Society, Inc.

The Eclipse Bicycle Company in Elmira Heights. They manufactured bicycles from 1895 until 1899 when they began to specialize in coaster brakes Courtesy of Chemung County Historical Society, Inc.

female boarding house to encourage young women to come work in the cloth and knitting mills. In 1896, 1,500 residents of this new community organized a village government and selected the name Elmira Heights.

The village was instrumental in the county's economic growth during the late 19th century and early 20th century. Scores of immigrants came to the area to work in the new factories in Elmira Heights and in other parts of the city. Throughout the 19th century, three immigrant groups had dominated the local economy: English, Irish/Scots-Irish, and Germans. But as the century closed, new groups of immigrants also made Chemung County their home. The heaviest influx of immigrants (primarily Jews, Italians, and Poles) began about 1880 and lasted until about 1920. African Americans continued to migrate from the South, and by 1920, the African-American population was triple what it had been in 1850. Each of the groups who came to the city during this period typically settled among its own kind, thus creating ethnic neighborhoods where residents could share places of work, places of worship, and a common language.

Italians came to Elmira in large numbers after 1880. By 1910, about 2,000 people of Italian origin or descent lived in the Elmira area. Eastern European immigration brought mostly Poles to Elmira, but there were also Ukrainians, Russians, Czechoslovakians, and Hungarians. Irish immigrants came in several waves throughout the 19th nineteenth century and formed perhaps the largest ethnic presence in the city. Compared to Italians and Poles, Jews came in relatively small numbers. At the beginning of the 20th century they occupied a six-block area on the east side of Elmira. German, Russian, and Eastern European Jews continued to arrive until the early 1920s, when the immigration quota acts restricted the flow of immigrants from southern and eastern Europe.

Many of these newcomers opened small businesses like groceries, tailor shops, and barber shops, while others worked in the mills and factories. Elmira Heights was not the only site of factories in the Elmira area. The American LaFrance Company manufactured fire apparatus such as steamers and hose carts at the turn-of-the-century and, by the 1920s, fire engines. The Elmira Iron and Steel Rolling Mill Company began in 1869, producing 20,000 tons of rails each year. J. Richardson and Company, shoe and boot manufacturers, opened in 1861 and continued in business until the early 20th century. They provided company housing for employees as well as executives. In 1912, Thatcher Glass Manufacturing Company opened a factory in Elmira to produce milk bottles and other glass containers. All of these companies, along with many others, provided jobs for the residents of Chemung County and attracted new immigrants.

Developments in transportation and an improved infrastructure aided the county's economic expansion. After the Civil War, the more efficient railway system caused shipping on the Chemung Canal to decline, and the canal closed permanently in 1878. In addition to improved transportation, the railroads provided employment. The Delaware, Lackawanna, and Western Railroad (DL&W) arrived in Elmira in 1882, connecting Buffalo to the East Coast. The Northern Central Railroad, the Pullman Company, and, later, the Pennsylvania Railroad each had shops in Elmira. By 1929, almost 2,500 Elmirans were employed by the railroads. Many smaller railroads covered shorter distances between Elmira and nearby towns like Corning, Ithaca, and Cortland.

Local trolley service began in 1871 with the creation of the Elmira and Horseheads railway, connecting the two towns. In the late 1880s, trolley lines reached Elmira's southside. Initially horses pulled the cars along the tracks, but by 1893, electric cars had replaced horse-drawn vehicles. In 1900, the area's two trolley companies merged to form the Elmira Water, Light, and Railroad Company. The trolley system reached its peak in the 1910s, declining when automobiles began to dominate the streets in the 1920s.

With the new industrial age and urban culture came a more pronounced need for open space and recreational activity. Economic growth and progress also meant that factories polluted the air and water, and people lived in close quarters. This

threat to physical health and well-being led to a nationwide movement to create more urban parks.

Elmira had two of the best known parks in New York's Southern Tier. Eldridge Park was one of the first landscaped parks in the Chemung Valley. Following the Civil War, Dr. Edwin Eldridge developed several hundred acres of swampland north of the Elmira city limits. By 1870, he had installed a small lake, fountains, classical statues, pagodas, and bridges along with an abundance of trees and plants. The 1870s saw the addition of a five-story "casino" that housed a restaurant, ice cream parlor, observation deck, and space for an orchestra. The trolley lines were extended to the park as was the line for the DL&W railroad, making travel to the park

very convenient. The City of Elmira purchased Eldridge Park in 1889 for $37,500 and, in the early 20th century, transformed it into an amusement park. After World War I there was a carousel, miniature railroad, roller coaster, small zoo, penny arcade, and shooting gallery. Roving photographers, glass engravers, and puppeteers provided other entertainment.

Rorick's Glen was the rival to Eldridge Park. Located on the south banks of the Chemung River, visitors reached the Glen by riding to the end of the trolley line along West Water Street then crossing a foot bridge spanning the river. In 1901, Rorick's Glen became home to one of the first summer theaters in the United States—a device created to increase travel on the streetcars. The theater was open on three

sides with canvas shades serving as walls. There was also a restaurant, miniature railroad with steam engine, roller coaster, and giant swing. Visitors could rent burros for trail riding during the day then spend their evening in the park's dance hall. Although the theater closed in 1917, Rorick's Glen's other attractions remained for several decades.

During the first three decades of the 20th century, the population of Elmira and Chemung County continued to grow thanks to a solid industrial base. From 1890 to 1930, the population in Elmira alone increased by 53 percent to 47,397. This was the last period of sustained prosperity for Chemung County. The 1930s would see the area's first decline in population. ❧

A trainload of American LaFrance steamers prepared for shipment, c. 1904-1913 Courtesy of Chemung County Historical Society, Inc.

Rorick's Glen, located on the south banks of the Chemung River, became home to one of the first summer theaters (pictured left) in the United States. Courtesy of Chemung County Historical Society, Inc.

The five-story "casino" at Eldridge Park housed a restaurant, ice cream parlor, observation deck, and space for an orchestra. Courtesy of Chemung County Historical Society, Inc.

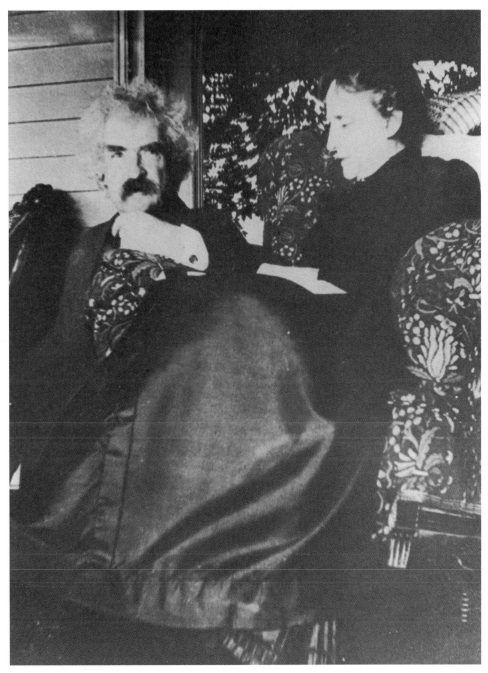

Samuel Clemens (Mark Twain) and Olivia Langdon Clemens on the porch of Quarry Farm, their summer retreat in Elmira, 1903. After their marriage in 1870, the Clemenses spent more than twenty summers here at the home of Twain's sister-in-law Susan Langdon Crane. In a detached octagonal study on the farm's property, Twain wrote some of his best known novels including: the Adventures of Tom Sawyer, Adventures of Huckleberry Finn, and The Prince and the Pauper. His time in Elmira became crucial to Twain's creative genius. Here he met and lived alongside former slaves, workers on the Underground Railroad, and activists like Frederick Douglass. These contacts helped shape Twain's views on slavery and racism. Since 1982, Quarry Farm, in an agreement with Elmira College, has been used as a temporary home for scholars of Mark Twain. Their work has been instrumental in redefining our understanding of the Clemenses' lives in Elmira. Courtesy of The Mark Twain House, Hartford, CT.

Chapter 5

DEPRESSION & WAR

A view of the Regent Theater on Water Street, looking northeast from Railroad Avenue, c. 1930. Courtesy of New York State Archives, State Education Department, Albany, New York.

As in the rest of the country, the 1930s did not start well in Chemung County. The crash of the stock market in October 1929 had signaled the beginning of the Great Depression. Welfare problems in the county grew during 1930, while private organizations, like the newly formed Catholic Charities, helped relieve the burden on local government. By the end of 1931, the City of Elmira was insolvent and could not pay its employees for the month of December. The fire and police departments went without paychecks for several months, and by mid-1932, they were forced to take a ten percent pay cut. The city's teachers also took a cut in pay. Elmira College, a school that had established itself as a strong women's college in the mid-19th century, eliminated several faculty members for the fall of 1932, while student enrollment fell 50 percent.

When President Franklin Roosevelt took office in March 1933, one of his first actions was to close the banks for four days to prevent massive withdrawals. New York's governor had already closed the state's banks for two days prior. Chemung County's banks managed to remain solvent and reopened following the bank holiday. Not all was good

Employment line at the opening of the Precision Tool Company in 1935. The company eventually became an office machines division of Remington Rand.

news for local commerce, however; several retail stores went out of business during 1933.

A further blow to the local economy came in 1934 when the Willys-Morrow plant on South Main Street in Elmira shut down. In a move that echoed the initial days of Elmira Heights, local citizens joined together to create a corporation called Elmira Industries, Inc. to take control of the abandoned Willys-Morrow plant. They raised enough money to purchase the site in 1935 and transferred it to the Precision Tool Company which later became an office machines division of Remington Rand.

The lower wages for municipal employees and losses in other business continued, but in 1937, the city managers restored full salaries. In the meantime, the city and the county made every effort to obtain as much federal aid as possible. Several of President Roosevelt's new relief agencies provided local jobs through improvement projects. Beginning in 1933, the Civilian Conservation Corps (CCC) hired young men at $30 a month to do forestry work at camps in Big Flats, Van Etten, and the Newtown Battlefield Reservation. In late 1933, the Civil Works Administration (CWA) provided jobs for 800 men when it granted $200,000 for improvements to infrastructure. Between 1933 and 1937, the Works Progress Administration (WPA) provided funding for construction of a sewage disposal plant, flood protection work on Newtown Creek, and repairs to river dikes. The WPA also funded construction of a municipal golf course and, together with the Public Works Administration (PWA), a new municipal stadium to be called Dunn Field. In 1938, the PWA provided funds for two new school buildings, additions to an existing school, and a new bridge over the Chemung River at Madison Avenue.

One of the largest local construction projects during the Depression was the elevation of the railroad tracks throughout Chemung County. The design goal eliminated at-grade crossings dangerous to drivers and pedestrians and alleviated traffic delays caused by slow freight trains. The largest part of the project was a 1,600-foot long concrete viaduct through downtown Elmira. Construction began in 1932 and was mostly funded by the federal government, the railroads, and New York State. The downtown viaduct opened in October 1934, and the remaining elevations

American LaFrance contributed to the WWII effort in Chemung County by manufacturing army trucks. Courtesy of Chemung County Historical Society, Inc.

Langdon family home at the northwest corner of Church and Main Streets in Elmira. Built in 1850 by Anson Ely, it was purchased in 1865 by Jervis Langdon, father-in-law of Mark Twain. The house was the site of Twain's marriage to Olivia Langdon and represented one of the area's most prominent families. In 1939, when the nation was just coming out of the Depression, Langdon's grandson offered the house to the City of Elmira for use as a museum. The city estimated the cost of adapting the house would be $57,000, which many leaders felt was too prohibitive. To gauge the opinion of taxpayers, the city published a ballot in the Star-Gazette explaining that accepting the Langdon home would mean a tax increase. The result was a vote opposed to keeping the house by an almost two-to-one ratio. The home was torn down and a shopping plaza was built in its place. Courtesy of Chemung County Historical Society, Inc.

were completed by 1937. The project created jobs for many people, but also provided Elmira with a bold and modern structure reflecting the streamlined styles of the 1930s. Other actions taken by the City Council to deal with the growing number of cars in Elmira included raising the city speed limit to 30 miles per hour in 1936 and the introduction of parking meters in 1940.

The radio industry had taken off in the early 1920s with the commercial production of home radio sets. By 1929, following the creation of two national networks, the sale of radio equipment reached $411 million. Elmira's first radio station, WESG, went on the air in 1932. The Elmira *Star-Gazette* newspaper leased the station from Cornell University and established studios on the top floor of the Mark Twain Hotel on Gray Street. In 1939, control of the station returned to Cornell when the *Star-Gazette* formed its own station, WENY, and built a transmitter east of Dunn Field on Elmira's southside. The new station broadcast music, news, and coverage of local semi-pro baseball games.

In December 1941, the publisher and general manager of the *Star-Gazette*, Frank Tripp, was serving as radio host for the annual fundraising appeal of the Arctic League charity organization when he was forced to break the news that the Japanese had attacked Pearl Harbor. By the time Congress declared war on December 11th, as many as 1,300 people in Chemung County had registered for civil defense. The local train stations soon became the embarkation point for many citizens going off to war.

As soldiers went to war in Europe and the Pacific, the people of Chemung County went to work on the home front to aid the war effort. The county's manufacturing concerns converted to war production. As early as 1938, the Eclipse Machine Division of Bendix Aviation Corporation had been designated to produce an aircraft cannon, but when World War II began, the plant went into mass production of fuses used to

explode anti-aircraft shells. The Remington Rand plant made parts for revolvers and other weapons, in addition to its business machines. American LaFrance, by this time Ward LaFrance, produced pontoon bridge trucks and recovery wreckers for military tanks. By 1943, Elmira Foundry was making steel castings for grenades and aluminum castings for planes, and the Elmira Knitting Mills were supplying the military with white, khaki, and olive T-shirts. The Navy took over a division of Remington Rand in November 1943 to facilitate production of the Norden bombsight.

In January 1942, Chemung County held its first trial blackout, and by decree of the Governor of New York, tire rationing went into effect. Food rationing began with sugar in April 1942 and expanded to include coffee, fruits, vegetables, meats, cheese, butter, and canned goods. In May, gasoline went on the ration list and, for most drivers, was limited to three or four gallons a week.

The former Civilian Conservation Corps (CCC) camp in Big Flats became the site of the Civilian Public Service camp for conscientious objectors in 1942. Participants worked on experimental grass and tree nurseries for the Soil Conservation Service. Courtesy of Swarthmore College Peace Collection, Swarthmore, PA.

Horseheads became a strategic warehousing site at the end of 1942, when 700 acres were set aside for the Elmira Holding and Reconsignment Point for storage of tanks, trucks, artillery, and amphibious landing craft. At Harris Hill, the Elmira Soaring Corporation conducted the first military glider training for Army Air Corps officers. Women participated in the local war effort by joining the Women's Army Auxiliary Corps, the Women's Ambulance and Defense Corps, and other service organizations. Women were also well represented in the manufacturing work forces at plants like Eclipse and Remington Rand.

More than 200 German and Italian prisoners of war were assigned to the Holding and Reconsignment Point in Horseheads in August 1944. They were housed in army tents and given recreation privileges such as attending movies at the local cinema.

In contrast, the wartime version of the CCC, the Civilian Public Service (CPS), set up camp in Big Flats. The CPS was an organization for conscientious objectors (those who resisted the draft on the basis of conscience and principal). The federal government required military draftees who could not serve due to religious beliefs to perform civilian duties of national importance, and

These women participated in the local war effort by joining the Women's Ambulance and Defense Corps (WADC). Courtesy of the Chemung County Historical Society, Inc.

WWII soldiers in training at the New York State Armory on Church Street in Elmira. Courtesy of Chemung County Historical Society, Inc.

the CPS provided a way to fulfill this obligation. Conservation work was the primary focus of the organization. The former CCC camp in Big Flats became the site for the new conscientious objectors camp in August 1942. Participants worked for the Soil Conservation Service on experimental grass and tree nurseries and related projects in Big Flats and Painted Post. After 1943, the Big Flats camp served as a reception center where inductees underwent a training period before receiving their permanent assignments.

By the end of World War II, thousands of people had migrated to Chemung County to work in the many wartime industries. Local farms suffered because young farm workers sought higher paying manufacturing jobs. In late 1945 and 1946, as 10,000 Chemung County citizens returned home from the war, industries returned to peacetime production. Soldiers found a strong economy at home as the repeal of wartime taxes increased spending and consumer demand kept factories at high production levels.

Chemung County, along with the rest of the nation, was on the cusp of a new era defined by people's experiences of war and a growing economy. ✌

Chapter 6

BECOMING A
MODERN COMMUNITY

Chemung County turns out for its sesquicentennial celebration on the courthouse lawn in Elmira, 1986. Courtesy of Chemung County Historical Society, Inc.

As air traffic increased in the 1960s, the Chemung County Airport underwent major improvements to the runways and the terminal building, photo c. 1965. Courtesy of Chemung County Historical Society, Inc.

Following World War II, Chemung County's suburbs expanded to accommodate new families and businesses. Several factors facilitated this growth, including transportation improvements and the GI Bill, which allowed returning servicemen to get loans to purchase new homes. This created a boom in new home construction, typically in the Colonial Revival and Tudor Revival styles. The growth of suburban residential areas also helped to bring modernization to rural schools.

The construction of the Southern Tier Expressway, a reconstruction and relocation of New York Route 17, further encouraged suburban growth. Access to the highway and the availability of cheap land allowed development of industrial parks and shopping centers in Horseheads. By 1960, the population of Chemung County reached 98,706, while Elmira's population dropped by nearly six and a half percent from a high of 49,716 in 1950, reflecting the flight from the urban center. The county's population growth in the 1950s prompted the consolidation of the Horseheads Central School District, mean-

ing money for larger school buildings and the end of one-room schoolhouses in Chemung County.

As the suburbs expanded, Elmira focused its policies towards replacement and refinement of its existing structures. The city created housing for ex-servicemen at Veterans Court, and, in 1953, completed the Jones Court housing project as a way to clean up the blighted neighborhood at Dickenson and Fourth Streets. Many residential areas on the periphery of downtown were rezoned for retail businesses.

The decades following World War II also saw the decline of the railroads. In 1956, the Pennsylvania Railroad discontinued passenger service in the area. In 1959, the Erie and Lackawanna railroads merged, leaving only one passenger station in Elmira serving 14 passenger trains each day. Passenger service declined in the 1960s, and by the middle of the decade the railroad determined it was losing more than one million dollars a year. The Erie-Lackawanna's famed passenger train, *The Phoebe Snow*, made its last stop in Elmira in January 1970.

Changes in lifestyle during the postwar era included the dawn of the television age. In 1950, the first television transmission to reach Chemung County came from Binghamton. By 1953, the valley had its own station, WTVE—Channel 24. Later that year it was joined by WECT—Channel 18—just in time to view baseball's World Series. Weather and financial difficulties forced the two stations off the air in 1954, but two years later both stations re-appeared (WECT had become WSYE, the satellite of a Syracuse station). Television changed the way people spent their leisure time, and several of Elmira's downtown theaters closed during this period.

The Chemung County Airport had opened in 1933 and was briefly served by American Airlines. In 1940, the airport had been designated a Defense Landing Area and became a major transportation hub during the war. By the 1950s, the airport had three airlines serving Chemung County passengers. As air traffic increased in the 1960s, the airport underwent major improvements to the runways and the terminal building.

Elmira continued to make improvements using the principals of urban renewal and funding from federal and state governments. The city established municipal parking lots and parking garages to deal with the growing number of cars. In 1969, Elmira undertook an ambitious slum-clearance project east of downtown by building 200 low-rise housing units with dollars from the United States Department of Housing and Urban Development. In the same area, the city constructed an eleven-story apartment tower for elderly residents.

Heritage Park government housing development on the east side of Elmira. Courtesy of Chemung County Historical Society, Inc.

Following a national trend that affected urban areas, one of the bigger threats to Elmira's downtown came in 1967, with the development of a shopping mall in Horseheads. Starting with 30 stores, including Sears and J.C. Penney, the suburban mall would lure shoppers away from the traditional downtown retail district. During the 1970s, the city tried in vain to attract shoppers back to downtown by constructing two new parking garages.

The event that changed Chemung County, and especially Elmira, more than any other in the 20th century was the 1972 Hurricane Agnes flood. Four days of rain in June resulted in the worst flood in Elmira's history. More than 15,000 people in Chemung County were evacuated from their homes. The waters swept away three bridges over the Chemung River

and severely damaged two others. The downtown post office had a water line 64 inches above the street level. The river crested at 31.4 feet in the Town of Chemung.

The flood brought millions of dollars' worth of damage to Elmira's downtown business district. Department stores like Sears and Iszard each suffered losses in the range of one million dollars. High water shattered store windows and merchandise floated through the streets. The city quickly put together an urban renewal-disaster relief proposal for approval in Washington. The project, known as the New Elmira Plan, called for the demolition of nearly 1,000 buildings in Elmira. After some alterations, the plan was approved in 1973 and, with $55 million from the federal government and another $10 million from New York State, large-scale urban renewal got underway.

The Plan called for the demolition of several blocks of retail and office buildings along the river facing East Water Street. Removal of these buildings, long considered eyesores, made way for the Mark Twain Riverfront Park. In all, the New Elmira Plan cleared over 40 percent of the city's commercial space.

Another significant feature of the new plan was the creation of a north-south artery connecting Southport and Route 14 with Horseheads and Routes 17 and 13. Approved in 1974, very little of the artery had been completed before 1990. The new road, Clemens Center Parkway, turned State Street into a four-lane divided highway. Removal of buildings along the west side of the street allowed for expansion of the old Keeney Theater which became known as the Clemens Center for the Performing Arts.

Clemens Center Parkway (shown at center of photo) as it crosses the Chemung River and heads north through downtown Elmira. Courtesy of Chemung County Historical Society, Inc.

By the mid-1990s, downtown Elmira had lost most of its retail establishments. As the new millenium approaches, the city continues its efforts to attract more businesses to downtown in the face of stiff competition from suburban malls in Big Flats. The flagship of the city's current master plan is a multi-purpose arena to be built on Main Street. Community leaders hope that activities such as sporting events, concerts, and conventions will draw visitors and retailers back to the downtown area.

Today the Chemung County Chamber of Commerce works to encourage local leaders to pursue a sustained, strong economy char-acterized by a diversity of employers in the manufacturing, retail, and service industries. The economy is growing rapidly in Big Flats with new housing, retail businesses, and industry, for example, the recent relocation of the headquarters of Corning Consumer Products to Chemung County's airport corporate park.

Improvements in transportation will make the county more accessible to visitors, resi-dents, and businesses alike. Congress has already approved the conversion of Route 17 into the future Interstate-86, and plans are underway to eliminate at-grade intersections along that highway. More sections of Clemens Center Parkway were completed as recently as 1999, bringing the downtown artery closer to achieving its intended destination. Working in concert, the two roadways will accommodate future expansion.

The area has changed dramatically in the decades since World War II. Local citizens are proud of the county's burgeoning economic growth. Recovery from the devastating effects of the flood of 1972 has demonstrated the tenacious spirit and perseverance of the peo-ple of Chemung County, and they are excited about the possibilities for the 21st century. ✑

Football star Ernie Davis, c. 1960. In high school, Elmira native Ernie Davis was voted All-American in both football and basketball at Elmira Free Academy. After graduating, he went on to play football at Syracuse University where he was voted All-American and, in 1961, became the first African American to win the coveted Heisman Trophy. Following college he signed with the Cleveland Browns, but was soon diagnosed with leukemia. He died in 1962 at the age of 22 without ever playing a profes-sional game. Today Elmira honors him with the Ernie Davis Community Center, Ernie Davis Middle School, and a commemorative statue. Courtesy of Chemung County Historical Society, Inc.

THE FLOOD OF 1972

*Above: Water Street during the Flood of 1972. Courtesy of Chemung County Historical Society, Inc.
Left: The event that changed Chemung County-and especially Elmira-more than any other in the
20th century was the Flood of 1972, caused by Hurricane Agnes. Pictured here is a view of
Elmira's flooded east side. Courtesy of Chemung County Historical Society, Inc.*

These buildings on the south side of Water Street were demolished following the Flood of 1972,
making way for Mark Twain Riverfront Park. Courtesy of Chemung County Historical Society, Inc.

Water Street, between Main Street and Railroad Avenue, as seen from Riverfront Park. The fabric of Elmira continues to change as we stand on the threshold of the new millennium. Courtesy of Chemung County Historical Society, Inc.

Partners in Progress

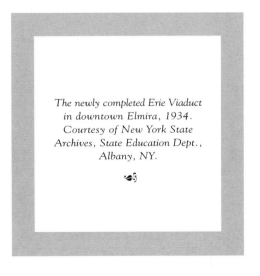

The newly completed Erie Viaduct in downtown Elmira, 1934. Courtesy of New York State Archives, State Education Dept., Albany, NY.

Chemung Canal Trust Company

*I*t was 1833 and State Senator John G. McDowell felt it was time to introduce legislation allowing the formation of a bank in the Village of Elmira, part of the area he represented. There were a few opposing lawmakers who hooted that they saw no need for such legislation.

"Why do you need a bank in Elmira when there's one in Albany?" they asked.

McDowell wasn't to be dissuaded. Of sturdy stock, his father, Daniel, had been part of General Sullivan's expedition to rout the Indians. The senior McDowell had been captured, had survived running the gauntlet, and had returned to settle in the area. Sen. McDowell and other forward thinkers knew the time was right. The Chemung Canal had just opened, connecting Elmira with Seneca Lake. Lumber, coal, and tobacco were being transported out of the area, and money was pouring in. Doing business some 300 miles away was no longer acceptable. His will prevailed, and the Chemung Canal Bank was chartered as the first financial institution in central New York.

Financing the start of the bank was not a problem. Community support was so strong that a stock subscription to raise $200,000 was closed after two days with staggering results: 704 persons had pledged $1,434,450 in stock—or seven times what they needed.

That first rush of enthusiasm has prevailed throughout the bank's history. Since that initial subscription, the bank's assets have climbed in 1998 to $600 million. Its Trust Department business tops $1.3 billion. A full complement of commercial and loan services are offered to clients through 14 branch offices, including the one in its main office in the modern elliptical six-story building at One Chemung Plaza on E. Water Street.

The bank remains one of the largest independent financial institutions in south central New York State. President Jan Updegraff and other bank officials intend to

Employees of Chemung Canal Trust Company in 1920 on the last day of business at its original main office.

keep it that way, constantly eyeing growth areas with expansion in mind, as other smaller institutions succumb to merger pressure.

"A critical element of our mission is to remain independent. Without that, everything else falls," Updegraff said.

Updegraff and other bank leaders glow when they recall battling and winning the one serious hostile takeover attempt by Northstar Bank in 1986. At that time, Chemung Canal Trust Co. was under the administration of president Boyd McDowell II, great-great-grandson of the first president. It was a David-and-Goliath clash in which McDowell and others mobilized loyal shareholders who were poised to reject a 2 1/2-for-1 share exchange proposal, when Northstar conceded.

This defiant independence was in the spirit of the bank's early leaders, giants of the day whose names are still intertwined in the history and cultural structure of the

community. Under their leadership, the bank helped establish many businesses: rolling and knitting mills, boat and bridge builders, and railroads. This commerce further enhanced the Southern Tier's foothold as a commercial hub.

When the bank opened, Andrew Jackson was president and there were 24 states. Stagecoaches were the way to travel, and bartering was the way to do business. The bank was an immediate success. Its first permanent headquarters in 1834 was at 413-415 E. Water Street, now the home of the Chemung County Historical Society. Traditionally, cashiers of the day, including John Arnot Sr., lived at the bank. Transactions were laboriously copied in ledgers in pen and ink.

Arnot, the bank's third president, is generally considered to have had the greatest influence on the bank's early development. A Scotsman who came to Elmira in 1819,

Arnot was noted for his business acumen, and within 10 years had outpaced other established merchants. He served as president in 1842-43, and again from 1857-73, having bought control of the bank in the 1850s. He and his sons, Steven T., John Jr., and Matthias H. Arnot, owned the bank for 46 years.

By 1839, the population of Elmira climbed to about 4,000, and a plank road brought in trade from Pennsylvania. The coming of the Erie Railroad in 1849, as well as smaller lines, brought further growth and glamour to the Southern Tier, launching it as a shopping and entertainment center. The second half of the 1800s marked a major growth period for the Southern Tier and the bank. The Chemung Canal Bank continued to play a vital role, advising and making loans for business and institutional expansion. The Elmira Female Seminary, now Elmira

College, was founded in 1855, followed by Elmira's first YMCA in 1858 and the Elmira Water Company in 1859.

Elmira, a staging center during the Civil War, hummed during and after the war, as did the fortunes of the bank. Tobacco had become a major crop, and two iron bridges, at Main Street and Lake Street, spanned the Chemung River to the fast-growing Southport population. The turn of the century brought tremendous advances—electricity, the telephone, the cash register, motion pictures—and the Chemung Canal Bank continued to expand. Noted writer Mark Twain, married to Elmiran Olivia Langdon, was a familiar figure on the streets and may have been a bank client. Elmiran David B. Hill, lieutenant governor with Grover Cleveland, became governor when Cleveland was elected president in 1884.

With railroads handling most of the

commerce, the Chemung Canal closed in 1873, the same year that John Arnot died after serving the bank and the community so diligently for more than 40 years. Business flourished, as did the cultural life of the community. In 1899, Elmira's first automobile, owned by Dr. William Fisher, startled people and horses alike. As automobiles became more popular, police worried that they were speeding along at the rate of 10 miles an hour. Elmira got its own sales company in 1910, when John N. Willys opened the Willys Morrow plant to begin manufacturing cars.

By then, Chemung Canal Bank was a public institution. The Arnots had terminated private ownership, and in 1902, the Elmira Trust Co. was formed, merging with the Chemung Canal Bank in 1903 to become the Chemung Canal Trust Company. Local industry continued to grow with bank support. Thatcher Manufacturing Co., Kennedy Valve Manufacturing Co., and Hilliard Clutch Co. moved to Elmira. Chemung Canal Trust Co. became widely known as a sound, growing financial institution. It was in 1925 that the bank moved to an imposing granite and marble building at the northeast corner of State and E. Water Streets, where it remained until the current modern structure was built in 1971.

The early and mid-1900s were marked by both wartime prosperity and peacetime slumps. The 1920s brought the new Keeney Theater (later, the Clemens Center), the opening of the Mark Twain Hotel, and the dedication of the city's first airport on the Southside. It was also the era of the stock market crash of 1929 and the deep depression that followed. To prevent panic and give the banks time to clarify their positions, President Franklin D. Roosevelt declared a bank holiday in 1933. Chemung Canal Trust was one of the few to open its doors the next day. In fact, it was so strong that it was able to make sizeable loans to faltering banks

Chemung Canal Trust Company Employees in the 1933 National Recovery Act Parade, celebrating the 100th anniversary of the bank.

in the area and in New York City.

The difficult period saw the close of the Willys Morrow plant, but construction jobs helped relieve some of the strain. The Chemung Canal Trust helped, directly funding jobs by giving the city $10,000. It also helped indirectly with participation in Elmira Industries, a forerunner of Southern Tier Economic Growth, headed by Frederick Swan, bank president from 1925 to 1950. Under his leadership, the group raised enough money to buy the idle Morrow plant and turn it over to Remington Rand to bring employment back to the area.

The World War II era followed a similar pattern of ups and downs, but generally Elmira remained stable. Chemung Canal granted hundreds of mortgages for new homes, and supported the growth of automobile dealerships, malls, and shopping plazas. Then, the 1950s brought the threat of war with Korea, and the 1960s saw the emotionally charged Vietnam era. Development in the Southern Tier was extraordinary, with the Westinghouse Corp., Corning Glass, and the A&P building new plants. At the same time, other industries expanded, bringing high employment rates.

The 1970s brought a recession, inflation, high interest rates, and a widely fluctuating prime lending rate. Locally, the picture was compounded by the flood of June 1972. A wide core of the city was shut down, as more than six feet of water swept through the area, ruining or severely damaging thousands of homes and businesses. Included was the new, modern Chemung Canal building that had just opened nine months earlier. Its basement, housing its safety deposit area, archives, and storage area, was clogged with mud. At its Westside Branch, a rowboat that had been set up in the lobby to promote boat loans, slowly rose as four feet of water poured in.

Hard-hit homeowners and bankers alike dug out of the mud, and wives of staff

members loaned their mangle irons that were set up in the bank to dry and iron stock certificates and other important papers. Since no restaurants were open, the bank provided hundreds of sandwiches daily to downtown workers. But the bank's true community spirit was shown when it offered loan extensions without charge so that the threat of foreclosure would not be added to homeowners' woes.

Through it all, the Chemung Canal Trust Co. continued as an independent bank, playing a crucial role in every endeavor designed to make the region prosper. By the end of the Cold War, area development efforts, with the support of Southern Tier Economic Growth, spurred new business development, with Toshiba, ABB Traction, Arnot Mall, and the Consumer Square business area in Big Flats lowering unemployment levels and creating new prosperity in the Southern Tier.

Chemung Canal experienced a milestone growth period in 1994, adding to its expanding network by acquiring three branches from Columbia Savings & Loan, as well as the Owego National Bank. Its assets set a record for one year, climbing from $398 million to $494 million.

"We felt we needed to expand. We knew we had a commanding share of the market for services within our traditional area and that future growth had to come from areas we were not now servicing," said President Updegraff.

Owego, with loss of the IBM plant, was in a downturn. Now it's surging ahead dramatically. Bath, Watkins Glen, and Painted Post remain level, and Updegraff is optimistic and anticipates further expansion in developing areas.

"The key is location, location, location," he said, adding that expansion will come through attrition as well. "And there will be attrition."

Lobby of second main office, razed to make way for current modern building at Water Street and Clemens Parkway (formerly State Street).

banking industry, Updegraff sees Chemung Canal Trust Co. as a strong survivor that will continue to serve the community as an independent institution. Its annual contributions to area nonprofit causes total about $200,000. The bank also encourages its staff members to volunteer—on bank time—to efforts such as the United Way, hospitals, Chambers of Commerce, and a wide range of community endeavors that even include reading programs in schools and pediatric offices, and building Habitat for Humanity houses.

The importance of independence and community ties are stressed in the bank's mission statement:

—To ensure that the Chemung Canal Trust Company remains a strong and independent community bank.

—To enhance the value of our shareholders' investment through increased earnings and dividends.

—To develop and deliver quality financial services and maintain high standards of business ethics and community leadership.

—To seek out and respond to the credit needs of each economic level within the communities we serve.

—To provide a supportive and rewarding culture for our employees. ◄§

Current modern Chemung Canal Trust Company Building, opened in September of 1971, just before the flood of 1972.

While other banks may lose independence or merge and then close in consolidation, Chemung Canal Trust Co. remains in a strong position. By updating its techology every few years, the bank is ready for the year 2000. By then, Updegraff expects assets to rise to over $750 million.

"We know where we are, and we know what's working and what will work for the new millenium. As a financial institution, we are capable of positioning ourselves to anticipate and to meet most of the needs of our client base," he said.

Some aspects of the bank, however, are absolute constants. Although intense merger pressure has brought a contraction in the

Chemung County Historical Society

When the Chemung County Historical Society settled in its current headquarters in 1982, it couldn't have found a more appropriate setting. The massive structure at 415 East Water Street, rich in history, is the oldest commercial structure in downtown Elmira.

The building, built in 1833, was the first home of the Chemung Canal Bank. The "Banking Floor Gallery," once the bank lobby and the area where tellers conducted business, still has its original vaults and marble and terrazzo flooring. Today it is used as exhibition space. Elegant Ionic mahogany columns, put in place by renowned architects of the era, Pierce & Bickford, still stand.

The building, which formerly housed the old Elmira Chamber of Commerce, the Elmira Light and Gas Co., law firms, and real estate establishments, allowed the Historical Society to fulfill its long-held goals of preserving and exhibiting objects that will help the community understand and appreciate its heritage.

The Historical Society has occupied four different buildings since its formation in 1923. In 1945, it used a small office on the second floor of the former Steele Memorial Library on E. Church Street. Artifacts were packed in boxes and stashed on top of book files. Others were stored in the bell tower of the Chemung County Courthouse.

In 1953, the Historical Society was given use of a two-story brick structure at the northwest corner of Market and William Streets, formerly used as a health clinic. In 1964, the center's quarters changed to 304 William Street, where displays included a Native American room, a collection memorializing Ross Marvin (who participated in the 1909 Peary expedition to the North Pole), the Mark Twain room, and a children's toy and doll room.

Even in its cramped spaces, the museum continued to push for development, with volunteers working tirelessly. Frances Brayton and Asaph Hall were considered the "cofounders" of museum activities. Brayton's work in spearheading the development of traveling loan cases for schools was recognized by the American Association for State and Local History when the organization presented its Award of Merit to the Society for her work. Paul Ivory, the first paid professional director, was hired in 1968. The disastrous flood of 1972 brought a rush of volunteers to save the museum collections. One of these individuals, Margaret Clute, remained for more than 10 years as archivist, while Martha Kelsey Squires maintained the library and archive for researchers.

The Society also began to think of future needs. Expansion of community services and increasing visitor interest in local history brought the realization that more space was necessary. With Mrs. Clute and Lyman Gridley as cochairmen, more than $400,000 was raised to buy and to restore the old bank building which is listed on the National Register of Historic Places.

The building's grand opening came on May 15, 1982, with fanfare and festivities, vintage automobiles, nineteenth-century arts and crafts, and with ladies dressed in sunbonnets and aprons. Its theme was "Celebrate the Past," but it also brought realization that the museum could now properly exhibit artifacts that had been collected for decades.

"The new building more than doubled our space. Now we could do professional museum exhibits," said Constance B. Barone, museum director.

It provided a large storage area, public spaces for meetings, and further develop-

Water Street entrance.

ment of its popular traveling loan cases for area schools. It also allowed the Society to focus more intently on its mission to "collect, preserve, research, exhibit, and educate with those objects that will serve to illustrate the story of humanity and nature in this county."

By 1989, the trustees recognized the need to complete the facility. Another capital campaign, accelerated by a challenge grant from the National Endowment for the Humanities, raised more than $500,000 for renovations and additions by 1993. With additional space and renovations, the museum has become a cornerstone for downtown Elmira, providing quality educational programming for those seeking information about the Chemung Valley. In 1996, the Board of Trustees designated the name "Chemung Valley History Museum" to distinguish its museum operations. On any given day one might find Civil

War enthusiasts researching in the archive, out-of-town visitors viewing the *Community Album* exhibit, school students navigating the galleries with activity sheets on clip boards, or a newspaper reporter collecting material for a local news feature. In the 1990s, the museum's education department developed in-depth interdisciplinary school projects and continued to work collaboratively with area organizations and museums.

Growth and development continues. Since the 1960s, the staff has expanded to three full-time and seven part-time positions. There are more than 1,200 members across the country and in Canada. Accreditation was granted in 1986 by the American

Association of Museums, and professional reviews and assessments have been conducted over the years to help keep the museum operation current with professional practices. A key benefit to members is the quarterly *Chemung Historical Journal*, with its fascinating articles about local lore, started in 1955 with Thomas E. Byrne, retired county historian, editing its contents.

Included among museum honors are an Award of Merit from the American Association for State & Local History for the exhibit and programs *A Heritage Uncovered: The Black Experience in Upstate New York*; a Certificate of Commendation for the exhibit *Outsiders All: Nineteenth-Century Prisons,*

Mental Hospitals, and Asylums; and a National Award of Merit from the Retirement Research Foundation for the video *A Heritage Uncovered* and its subsequent showing on television's Public Broadcast System.

Through the years, long-term and temporary exhibitions, along with catalogs of the exhibitions as they change, continue to attest to the dedication and creativity of the museum's countless number of volunteers, trustees, and staff members. ◄§

The Howell Gallery houses temporary exhibitions at the Society's Chemung Valley History Museum on Water Street.

Chemung County Chamber of Commerce

At the beginning of the twentieth century, business and industry flourished in Chemung County to the point where Elmira was called the "Queen City of the Southern Tier." The downtown area was alive with clothing and dry goods stores, restaurants, and hotels. New wholesale firms and industries blossomed throughout the area.

The Chemung County Chamber of Commerce, a leading voice of business in the community since 1905, is a direct descendant of several groups that had earlier emerged to foster continued progress during that turn-of-the-century growth period. The maxim "In business for your business" applies to the Chamber today, just as it did in 1897, when the Board of Trade was established by a group of "solid and energetic" jobbers and manufacturers whose goal was continued commercial and industrial development.

The Elmira Industrial Association was formed in 1890 to promote growth in the new community that was to become Elmira Heights. In the city's commercial life, the Merchants' Association and the Business Men's Association were active. All these

Business leaders have many opportunities to network with each other at programs hosted by area Chamber members. These programs also allow participants to gain insight on the host's business.

The Chemung County Commerce Center, established in 1998, houses the Chamber of Commerce, Southern Tier Economic Growth, the Chemung County Planning Department, and several additional economic development and business assistance organizations.

groups merged in 1905 to become the Elmira Chamber of Commerce, supported by 125 merchants and manufacturers.

The group—variously called the Elmira Chamber of Commerce and the Elmira Association of Commerce before emerging under its current, more encompassing, title of Chemung County Chamber of Commerce—has been responsible for much of the growth through critical periods of the community's development. It supported the building of the elegant Mark Twain Hotel in 1928-29, pushed for the elevation of the Erie Railroad tracks in 1934, and was instrumental in 1936 in attracting to

Elmira the massive Remington Rand plant that at its peak employed more than 6,600 workers.

Through the years, the Chamber has changed with the times to focus on new issues and opportunities that affect the region's prosperity. Through efforts in such diverse areas as government regulations and legislation, small business concerns, tourism promotion, and economic development, the Chamber works daily to enhance the economic well-being and quality of life in Chemung County.

The Chamber channels its ongoing programs through three divisions: the Convention and Visitors Bureau, the Public Affairs Council, and the Member Services Council.

The organization's structure enables the Chamber to mobilize its powerful membership to champion any cause that will affect business—and living—in the community. This was demonstrated recently when local community, business, and legislative groups joined forces in a massive effort that brought the National Warplane Museum to Chemung County in 1998. The impressively integrated campaign convinced the museum,

In honor of its most celebrated resident, Chemung County is known as "Mark Twain Country." Samuel Clemens, a.k.a. Mark Twain, spent a great deal of time enjoying the views of the countryside which inspired several of his books that were written while he summered in Elmira.

formerly located in Geneseo, N.Y., that Chemung County would be the ideal location to house and display its collection of more than 100 classic military aircraft. The addition of the museum brings a new phase to Chemung County's enduring heritage of aviation interests. It also adds another chapter to the Chamber's long history of constructive involvement in flight. In 1930, the Chamber was the primary force in bringing to Elmira the first National Soaring Contest, an event that is still held periodically. Through the Chamber's support, Elmira became known as the "Soaring Capital of America" and the home of the National Soaring Museum.

The acquisition of the Warplane Museum helps attract thousands to the area for the annual Wings of Eagles Air Show. These initiations are tied closely to the Chamber's dynamic Tourism Convention and Visitors Bureau (CVB), which has been designated by the Chemung County legislature as the official tourism promotion agency for the county. In one of its most important functions, the CVB produces and distributes about 150,000 travel guides promoting the region by focusing on such attractions as

Elmira's legacy as the summer home of Mark Twain and some impressive Civil War history. The CVB also works with the Finger Lakes Association in marketing tourism on a regional basis.

One of the CVB's largest recent successes came by way of neighboring counties' motor racing's NASCAR. Race Week, a festive downtown Elmira celebration, is held in conjunction with the NASCAR Winston Cup race, which is run annually at Watkins Glen. With cars, drivers, and race memorabilia filling the downtown, Race Week quickly climbed to a prime annual attraction that draws more than 30,000 fans each year.

Members, as well as the community in general, also benefit directly from the legislative efforts of the Chamber's Public Affairs Council. It played an active role in 1995 on the statewide business coalition that successfully lobbied for a substantial cut in state business and personal income taxes. The Council also was highly visible in a statewide campaign for legislation that reduced by $63 per employee the amount of unemployment insurance paid by every business in the state. Advocacy efforts for state and federal funding also helped rekindle progress that had long been stalled on construction of a north-south arterial highway through Elmira.

Area firms have learned they can also count on help through the Member Services Council. The Council sprang into action in 1990 when problems began developing in a large contract to be awarded to ABB Traction from the Southeastern Pennsylvania Transportation Authority. ABB Traction appeared to be the lowest bidder, but questions arose in Pennsylvania about awarding such a lucrative contract to a company in another state. The problem was resolved when the Council was able to show reverse situations in which Pennsylvania firms had won New York State contracts.

In a popular and effective way of promot-

ing communications among businesses in the area, the Chamber sponsors "Business Before Business" and "Business After Business" sessions, bringing members together to exchange information in a social setting twice a month. The Chamber also has stepped up efforts to aid local businesses that want to explore the option of conducting trade on a global scale. It helps provide information by joining those new to international trade with more experienced local firms already operating in world markets.

The success of the Chamber's three-pronged structure is shown in its increased membership and enthusiasm of its participants. Membership has grown from 300 during a low period in 1983 to more than 900 in 1998. With a staff of 10, double that of 1985, the Chamber is located in the historic former Steele Memorial Library building at 400 East Church Street in Elmira. ❧

Visitors to the area can enjoy a 90-minute narrated trolley ride through historic Elmira. The trolley stops for a side tour through Mark Twain's Study and at the National Soaring Museum atop Harris Hill.

Arnot Ogden Medical Center

The three Civil War surgeons had seen the horrors of medical practice at the infamous Elmira Prison Camp, where more than 12,000 sick and injured soldiers were held in an atmosphere that bred malnutrition and disease. The war was over, but with frequent accidents at the Erie Railroad yards, it was still common practice to amputate limbs in boxcars that served as makeshift operating rooms.

The physicians, Drs. William C. Wey, Truman H. Squires, and Patrick Flood, decided to press for the development of a community hospital. The time was right. The small village

had grown into a transportation hub, drawing immigrants who were seeking their fortunes. But funding was scarce in the uncertain post-war economy, and their efforts failed.

The physicians refused to give up. Providentially, in 1887, a generous benefactor responded. Marianna Arnot Ogden, one of Dr. Wey's patients and the daughter of John Arnot, pioneer Elmira merchant and banker,

was drawn into the struggle. A wealthy socialite, at the age of 50 she had married William Butler Odgen, first mayor of Chicago and first president of the Union Pacific Railroad. Just two years after their marriage he died, and Dr. Wey convinced the grieving widow that building Elmira's first hospital would be a fitting tribute to her late husband.

Then she decided to honor her father also by including his name in the title. On December 22, 1888, the Arnot Ogden Memorial Hospital opened its doors with 25 beds and a staff of three physicians, two nurses, a matron, and four other employees. Through the years, expansion and progress have marked the development of the hospital. A name change to Arnot Ogden Medical Center reflects its growth to a four-floor, five-wing regional institution that has maintained cutting edge technology with services usually seen only at university hospitals. Its Finger

Lakes Heart Institute, Neonatal Intensive Care Unit, Health Center for Women, Falck Cancer Center, and other specialty programs attract patients from throughout central New York State and northern Pennsylvania.

The vision began with Mrs. Ogden's $75,000 grant that bought a single three-story building considered one of the finest hospital structures in the country at the time. It even contained a primitive air-conditioning system and gas and electric lights. Still, skeptical nurses carried kerosene lanterns on their rounds.

Further donations by the Arnot family—a total of $370,000 in endowments—as well as community fund drives kept the hospital going. People donated food, coal, and bed linens, and Dr. Wey came up with the idea of an alms box in the lobby. Once a month the board scooped out donations averaging $6 to $7 to help run the hospital.

The change in medical care has been profound. The first patient, Ella Bronson, 27, was admitted on Christmas Eve, 1888, with a condition characterized by excessive bleeding. She was discharged 100 days later with a single entry: Cured. At the turn of the century, wealthy patients received their care at home, pampered in sunlit rooms. Hospitals were considered refuges for the poor. Antiseptics and the theory that disease is spread by germs were just being debated. Even in Elmira's advanced new institution, surgery was routinely performed in hallways.

The hospital earned the respect of the community by pushing forward in its development. To ease the nursing shortage, a School of Nursing was established in September 1889, just in time to provide care for victims of a diptheria epidemic that swept Elmira. In 1894, at a cost of $590, Arnot Ogden purchased its first ambulance, a horse-drawn buggy stashed at the Jones Livery Stable on Market Street.

The hospital's development is highlighted by a number of "firsts." It was one of the first hospitals in New York State to provide

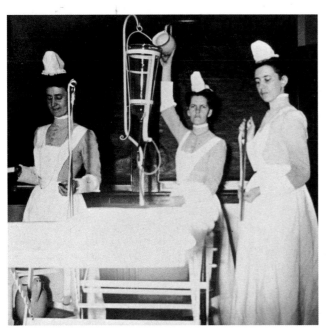

an X-ray apparatus, only two years after the discovery of X-ray technology in 1895, when even Buffalo's advanced facility did not have it. The first recovery room in New York State opened at Arnot Ogden in 1956, along with a new operating suite. In 1958, the hospital opened the first Intensive Care Unit in the state.

Arnot Ogden started its first major expansion in 1926. Dr. D. Hamilton Doxie Wey and Sarah Wey Tompkins, children of one of the hospital's founders, launched a $900,000 fund drive for construction of the C Wing. Housing the intensive care unit for the past 40 years, the wing is being renovated for the cardiac rehabilitation program.

In 1952, with staff members who had returned from World War II and the Korean War, the hospital was ready for another expansion. The second community appeal raised $1.5 million to replace the 1888 building and modernize the newer structures. The 1960s saw the beginning of development of major specialty centers, moving the hospital to the forefront in technological advancements. In 1964, electronic monitoring was introduced in the intensive care center. The 1970s focused on the development of centers specializing in cancer, heart disease, and neonatal intensive care.

In 1973 the cardiac surgical program began, evolving 25 years later into the Finger Lakes Heart Institute. The program consolidates cardiac services and integrates a full spectrum of patient care in a seamless framework that includes risk reduction, diagnostic and therapeutic cardiology, cardiac surgery, rehabilitation, and wellness. In 1986, the hospital was designated as one of two area trauma centers in the Rochester region, assuring sudden severe trauma victims of timely and appropriate care.

The next decade brought the Falck Cancer Center in 1991, the Health Center for Women in 1992, and the E wing in 1997, offering state-of-the-art ambulatory surgical and critical care environments, designed to address the increasing need for outpatient treatment and highly sophisticated inpatient care.

The hospital's continued growth has made it the second largest employer in Chemung County, with 1,400 employees. As with most hospitals, admissions have dropped with changing technology and the extensive shift to outpatient care.

Anthony J. Cooper, president and chief executive officer of the Arnot Ogden Medical Center, sees patients participating more actively in their own health care. The hospital's role will be largely one of providing the necessary tools, education, and positive feedback.

"The message is you can't just be passive. You can't just sit in a chair, have someone give you a pill, and you'll be cured. You have to diet, exercise, buckle your seat belt, stop smoking," Cooper said.

His vision is for Arnot Ogden to move closer to the patient, expanding into nearby areas such as Horseheads. He also sees the development of links with other health care providers, such as university-based facilities.

"Now, our principal mission is curing people," Cooper said. "As we go forward, we will be helping to prevent disease."

Elmira College

Coeducational since 1969, Elmira College was founded as the "mother of women's colleges," opening its doors in 1855 as the first college for women which offered a program of study and demanded degree requirements characterized by the same rigor and expectations of those at contemporary men's colleges.

A leading citizen of Elmira, Simeon Benjamin led the "Friends of Education," a group interested in higher education who recognized that few women of the day had an opportunity to attend college. Although Auburn, New York, was first considered the site for the unprecedented institution, Elmira was selected when Benjamin, an Elmira businessman, backed his preference with a generous founding gift.

Jervis Langdon is remembered as another of the college's founding trustees. His daughter, Olivia, was a member of the class of 1864 and later married Samuel Clemens, known world-wide as Mark Twain. The Clemenses vacationed in Elmira at Quarry Farm for 22 years. Comforted by the tranquillity of the nineteenth-century farm and inspired by the rich history of Elmira, Twain wrote many of his best-known novels, including his masterpiece, *Adventures of Huckleberry Finn*, in an octagonal study which overlooked the Chemung River.

Given to Elmira College by the Langdon family, the famous octagonal study now sits on the Elmira College campus, which has been described by the *Philadelphia Inquirer* as "picture postcard perfect" and stands as testimony to the college's long and rich history. Eight of the college's buildings are listed on the National Register of Historic Places. The octagonal Cowles Hall, the college's first building, still stands. Harris Hall was named for Dr. M. Anstice Harris, dean of the college from 1900 to 1930 and acting president in 1915. Hamilton Hall, recognized as one of the finest examples of English collegiate Gothic architecture in America, is named for Dr. W. Adelbert Hamilton, a professor and administrator from 1900 to 1939. Carnegie Hall was the gift of steel magnate Andrew Carnegie in 1911. The modern library, the campus center, and many of the dormitories were built from 1955 to 1975, under the inspirational leadership of the college's tenth President, J. Ralph Murray, L.H.D.

Members of the Elmira community founded Elmira College, and the community and college continue to enjoy an exemplary relationship. As an economic engine, Elmira College impacts the community to the effect of $60 million. As the only college in the nation to both give credit for and require all students to perform community service, Elmira College students help nonprofit and community organizations save approximately $80,000 each year. The college also requires each student to complete a field experience,

Statue of Simeon Benjamin, founder of Elmira College.

allowing community industries and agencies to whittle more than $330,000 from their operating budgets.

Elizabeth Dole, former director of the American Red Cross and Secretary of Transportation, said during her commencement speech in 1995 that Elmira College's dedication to community service "is not only meeting the need of higher learning, it is meeting the need of higher yearning."

Hundreds of college-sponsored events also help bond the college to the community. These include music and theater productions, art exhibits, and film and lecture series. The community also visits the Gannett-Tripp Library, which serves as the government repository for federal documents.

Members of the Elmira community seek college degrees at Elmira College in the evening, weekend, and summer academic programs. Each year, over 200 part-time undergraduate and graduate students earn Elmira College diplomas.

Early softball team at Elmira College.

The college is an integral member of the community as well as one of the top employers, notes Dr. Thomas Meier, college President. "We offer opportunities for our neighbors to expand and enhance their professional interests and relax with athletic and performing arts events," said Dr. Meier. "The college's campus is an asset to the community, as are the bright, energetic students enrolled at the college."

Under Dr. Meier's strategic leadership, the college has experienced remarkable growth. Enrollment has increased by more than 50 percent in the past decade, to more than 1,100, and prep school and high school valedictorians and salutatorians comprise 15 percent of the entire student body.

Students list the college's academic reputation, friendly atmosphere, and picturesque campus as top reasons for choosing the private, liberal arts college. The college's rich traditions unite the student body and develop a strong sense of pride and class spirit. The freshman experience begins with a four-day, nationally recognized orientation program that helps new students make the transition to college life. During orientation, students are introduced to a variety of Elmira College traditions, including freshman beanies, class Patron Saints, and singing college songs. Worn as a class symbol, freshman beanies help to unite the class, instill a sense of pride, and develop class spirit.

"Patron Saints" guide the class through their Elmira College experience. They welcome new students to the Elmira College family by presenting them with beanies; they encourage students, challenge them, and support them; and after four years of assistance and camaraderie, Patron Saints present members of their class with graduation hoods.

The fond tradition of singing dates to the college's founding. New students learn these songs, and a variety of other college tunes, during their first days on campus. In the early days, Elmira College students crafted the lyrics of songs to reflect their feelings toward world events. *Keep the Home Fires Burning*, the famous World War I song, was written by an Elmira College alumna, Lena Gilbert Ford, class of 1887. *Recollection's Magic Sway* embodies the strong sentiments early students held for their Alma Mater. Although extinct at many college campuses across the country, the "Alma Mater" is not only incorporated into every Elmira College event, but students also sing it while linking arms and swaying to the melody.

In the new millennium, Elmira College continues to provide a sound liberal arts education to a student body surrounded by history and innovation. In the nineteenth century, Mark Twain did his best work in Elmira; one may expect that Elmira College students will continue to do their best work in Elmira as well. ✑

Grounds of Elmira College.

Dalrymple Gravel and Contracting

*E*phriam Dalrymple was an adventurer. He had dabbled in gold mining out West and in lumbering in the Elmira and Galeton areas in the late 1800s. But when he inherited a portion of the large farm located between two creeks in Southport, he found the niche that led to the development of, what is now, one of the largest heavy and highway construction companies in the Northeast.

material for most of the area construction.

Business continued at a steady pace. Then in 1936, Ephriam's sons, Edward and Henry, envisioned further growth. They incorporated the company, expanding to provide construction services, as well as materials. Quickly, the firm grew to become a major, full service contracting corporation with capabilities for producing its own

ment," says David Dalrymple, one of the current company officials and a great-grandson of Ephriam Dalrymple.

The depression brought a temporary lull. Then President Roosevelt enacted Works Progress Administration legislation to provide employment for the needy and to boost the economy. Expanding its equipment, with steam shovels and steam rollers, Dalrymple's was in place and ready for road projects in New York and Northern Pennsylvania.

World War II brought another huge leap, with the urgent need for construction of such factory projects as Remington Rand, Bendix, and General Electric. Dalrymple's became a key player, supplying most of the concrete and doing the foundation work and site grading.

In the 1950s, the road business dramatically expanded with the initiation of the interstate highway system. The company, under the third generation leadership of Robert E. Dalrymple and Edward C. Dalrymple, began working in a multi-state area as the federal government injected massive funds into construction of the system that linked state highways throughout the country.

Area work continued with construction of such projects as the Patterson Bridge in Corning, the Elmira-Corning Regional Airport, and construction of many sections of Route 17. After the flood of 1972, the company worked around the clock to rebuild the Main Street Bridge, and later constructed the Clemens Parkway Bridge.

While many area residents perceive Dalrymple's largely as a paving company, it has long since moved into a three-state operation in a corridor running from Northern New York to Central Virginia. Company headquarters remains at its original site at the old Ephriam Dalrymple farm. But there are no indications—not even a sign posted—of the massive operation into which the company has evolved.

The business operates three concrete

Dalrymple workers during the early days.

The Dalrymple Gravel and Contracting Co. has continually expanded under the leadership of four generations of Dalrymples. It started at the turn of the century, when Ephriam Dalrymple discovered the need for sand and gravel for construction projects in the growing Elmira area. With a ready supply from the creek beds, he hitched up horse-drawn wagons, shoveled in the material, and headed for the sites. Soon he was supplying

crushed aggregate and concrete.

Always in the forefront, the Dalrymples, in 1938, erected a concrete plant to become one of the first companies in the state to provide ready mixed concrete, using a mixer mounted on a truck. Previously, sand and gravel were hauled to the site so that concrete could be mixed on the job.

"We take it for granted today but, at the time, it was a major technological advance-

plants, seven blacktop plants, and five aggregate pits and quarries in Upstate New York, Pennsylvania, and Virginia. Its own portable concrete and blacktop plants give the company the ability to provide on-site materials for large projects anywhere in the Northeast. Stored at various sites, are more than 1,000 pieces of equipment, including huge earth-movers, rollers and shovels, loaders, cranes, barges, and tugboats that are used in gigantic and complex projects that are considered in the "world class" category.

One of the most significant was the reconstruction of I-68 and I-95 Interchange, a $42-million job on the Washington, D.C. Beltway that took four years to complete. It was part of a $500-million-plus plan to improve U.S. Route 50 and speed suburban and beach-bound traffic. It included eliminating an old cloverleaf in favor of three new "flyovers." It also included widening the existing U.S. 50 bridge over I-95 and making a series of other road and bridge improvements.

Another major project was the $52 million Utica, New York project consisting of 15 composite girder bridges and the reconstruction of State Highways 5A, 5S, 8, 12, and I-790. Others included the $12.2-million contract for replacement of the Route 28 bridge over the Erie Canal, Herkimer, New York; and the $14.4-million three-pier bridge at Phoenix, New York.

Airport paving projects range far beyond Chemung County. They include projects at the Naval Air Station at Patuxent, Maryland; Dulles International Airport, Washington National Airport, Charlottesville, Virginia Airport, Link Field in Binghamton, Hancock Field in Syracuse, the Ithaca Airport, and the Erie, Pennsylvania Airport.

Dams and marine projects, including a $14-million system that involved a mechanical lift bridge over the Barge Canal, have also been built by the firm.

Today, David Dalrymple, his brother Robert H. Dalrymple, and their cousin

Edward C. Dalrymple Jr. are the principal officers of the business. They count among their key resources more than 50 engineers, project managers, superintendents, and administrators. With their skills and performance, the Dalrymple Gravel and Contracting Co. and its subsidiary, Chemung Contracting Corp., has won numerous "excellence" awards and earned the reputation for completing projects ahead of schedule on a regular basis.

One of the things the company prides itself on is the fact that, when it is exporting its skills and equipment for a $42-million job in Maryland, it is generating new money and jobs into the Elmira community. Dalrymple's has a steady staff of 325 employees, but that figure can rise to 600 when major construction projects are underway.

In a "high risk" operation, with the company's success resting on the bidding process and a shifting economy, David Dalrymple says the firm's goal is to remain a growing and viable business. That means the company must not only be the low bidder, but must be able to complete the project on time and for the stated price.

"When they open those bids in Albany, it doesn't matter who you know; you have to be the low bidder. That's the most challenging part: you've got to be able to prepare a bid for a very complex project and you have to make sure you can build it for that price," Dalrymple says. ❧

Part of the Washington DC Beltway constructed by Dalrymple, 1992.

Chemung County Aviation

On any given day, an air buff scanning the skies above the Elmira-Corning Regional Airport might see a scheduled airliner ready to take off, a helicopter flapping about the nearby Schweizer Aircraft Corp., or a sailplane bouncing off a thermal near the National Soaring Museum. Or, they might look with disbelieving eyes at a World War II B-17 on a passenger tour from the National Warplane Museum.

Aviation in Chemung County centers on activities at the airport, Schweizer's, and the two museums, which draw visitors from around the world. But the history of flight in Chemung County is firmly rooted in exploits by some of the field's most daring and colorful figures, from pioneer air mail pilot Leon "Windy" Smith to Elmira Astronaut Eileen Collins, the nation's first woman to command a space craft.

The airport started as a grassy strip for emergency landings in 1933. American Airlines constructed the site, inaugurating flights from the field on June 20, 1933. Air mail services started there in October 1934. Now the airport has about 25 air carrier operations a day, linking travelers via Pittsburgh, Philadelphia, New York City, and Detroit to countries throughout the world. The airport has grown to a 1,000-acre facility that now

National Soaring Museum.

houses 25 major corporations creating an economic impart of over $65 million a year.

The area's rich background in aviation includes some of the most flamboyant episodes in aviation history. There was the time that racing great, Barney Oldfield and daring aviator, Lincoln Beachey held a 200-mile-per-hour auto-air race in the Maple Avenue area. Then, in the 1920s famed aviator, Jimmy Doolittle, visited Elmira and thrilled onlookers by flying under the Main Street bridge in his fighter plane. And area residents have always been taken with the escapades of Leon "Windy" Smith of Pine City, a pioneer air mail pilot and barnstormer, who performed at fairs with female parachuters Ruth Blackman and Irene DeVere jumping from the wings of his plane.

The county's early history of flight centered on an airport at Caton Avenue in Southport, an 87-acre farm with an old tobacco barn that was converted into a hangar. Soaring activities in the area started nearby at South Mountain, where early pilots such as the Schweizer Brothers—Ernie, Paul, and Bill—gathered for some of the first contests.

Then, as the level land of Big Flats was found to be a better site for the airport, soaring pioneers discovered that updrafts from nearby Harris Hill were ideal for launching their aircraft. The National Glider Association (NGA), was formed in 1929, followed by the organization of the Soaring Society of America in 1932. Elmira was chosen as the site for the first national contest in 1930 by German soaring pioneer Wolfgang Klemperer. Interest grew and Elmira, Soaring Capital of America, was host to the first 13 national contests.

Hundreds of regional, national, and international contests have been held since 1932 on Harris Hill under the direction of

National Warplane Museum.

the Elmira Area Soaring Corp., now known as the Harris Hill Soaring Corp. Early contests attracted as many as 10,000 visitors.

In 1939, Schweizer Aircraft Corp. was formed, moving first into the Elmira Knitting Mills building in Elmira Heights, then to its Big Flats plant in March 1943. Between the close of World War II, when Schweizers produced many military and training gliders, and 1987, when glider production at Schweizer ceased, the company produced over 80 percent of the sailplanes made in the United States. Schweizers began construction of "Ag-Cat" agricultural aircraft in 1957, producing 2,646 before the business was sold in 1995.

Since 1987, Schweizer has moved into worldwide markets with a diverse product

Elmira-Corning Regional Airport.

base of innovative designs. This production includes helicopters for commercial, military, and police applications. It also includes special purpose reconnaissance aircraft, which possess unique operating features.

To document soaring activities across the country, the National Soaring Museum (NSM) was created in 1969. The museum holds more than 70 historically significant gliders and sailplanes, the largest collection in the world. It is the official document and memorabilia repository for the Soaring Society of America,

home to the U.S. Soaring Hall of Fame, and runs a myriad of educational programs for both students and adults.

One long-term NSM exhibit features Elmira Astronaut Eileen Collins, who became the first woman to pilot an American spacecraft (1995) and the first to command one (1999). As a child, she drew part of her inspiration to fly from watching gliders over Harris Hill, just as she is inspiring young women visitors to NSM to think of careers in aviation.

The NSM, the HHSC and its active gliderport, and Schweizer Aircraft and its Glider School and World War II glider training program, are among the reasons Elmira is considered "the Soaring Capital of America."

The most exciting new development in the area of aviation is the addition of the National Warplane Museum, which moved to the Elmira-Corning Regional Airport after outgrowing its quarters in Geneseo, New York. This world-class facility opened on July 15, 1998. During its first five months of operation, more than 18,000 visitors saw military aviation history come to life through a collection of changing exhibits, engines, and 25 vintage and modern aircraft from the 1930s through the 1970s.

The overall 115,000-square-foot building also is used for banquets and receptions, accommodating up to 800 guests in historic surroundings complemented by a staging kitchen for catering, gift shop, and multi-purpose theater.

Visitors may watch volunteers restore World War II-era planes to flying condition. One can walk under the wings of a sleek F-14 Tomcat in one of the two 30,000-square-foot

hangars. For an extra fee, generally from about May through November, one can propel oneself down memory lane with a nostalgic ride on the Museum's historic B-17 *Flying Fortress*, one of only a dozen still flying in the world. Known as the "Fuddy Duddy," the B-17 is the pride of the Museum's collection.

Home of the Wings of Eagles Air Show, the National Warplane Museum held its first air show here in 1997. The facility, open year round, is located off NYS Route 17, Exit 51. The Air Show generally attracts about 100,000 spectators.

Unlike situations at other museums, visitors who fly in to the Elmira-Corning Regional Airport can park their aircraft at the fixed base operation located immediately next to the museum. Upon exiting the FBO facility, one will find the museum within easy walking distance, the entrance being approximately 200 yards to the east.

It's part of an effort to make the airport more community oriented. The airport holds Fourth of July fireworks and a Ride for Pride motorcycle event, which winds up with about 1,000 bikes on the runway. The airport also cooperates with the Experimental Aircraft Association in providing as many free first rides for children as possible, having given thousands to date.

Normally, one only arrives at the airport to board a plane; Chemung County, however, offers more than that by structuring its airport as a major part of the community. ◄§

Elmira Star-Gazette

The *Elmira Star-Gazette* was born in a roisterous, boisterous era when settlers were still carving a community out of the wilderness, and chickens, pigs, and geese had the run of the streets. Horse-drawn wagons provided transportation, and bartering was the principal commerce of the day. A load of wood might buy a new dress, a pair of boots, or a year's subscription to the newspaper.

The newspaper, originally *The Gazette*, started in 1828. Owned by Job A. Smith, it was one of about a dozen competitors that bloomed as political organs and quickly faded. Then a chance stop in Elmira by Frank E. Gannett in 1906 sparked the growth of the publication. Gannett, an Ithaca newsman, was en route by train from Pittsburgh to Ithaca. He stopped for lunch at the old Langwell Hotel, where a friend told him a slice of the local paper might be for sale. Gannett missed the train and swung the deal, dickering with the owner, political power David B. Hill, former Democratic governor, U.S. senator, and thorn-in-the-side of President Grover Cleveland. To meet the $20,000 price, Gannett used his $3,000 savings, $7,000 borrowed from friends, and $10,000 in notes to Hill.

The money bought Gannett half interest with Erwin R. Davenport on June 6, 1906.

Through acquisition of *The Evening Star*, it became *The Star-Gazette* in 1907, the first step in a merger pattern that formed the Gannett Company Inc. Eighty-four newspapers throughout the country now comprise the company, including TV stations and *USA Today*, the country's first national newspaper.

Gannett not only bought the newspaper, but he also hired a young reporter named Frank Tripp, the first person he met when he entered the building. Tripp quickly moved to manager and publisher, a post he held for 42 years until his death in 1964. Gannett moved on to what became the company headquarters in Rochester. Tripp stayed in Elmira to achieve deep respect for his part in local growth and to attain a national reputation as a journalist.

The spirit of the two newspapermen permeated the early development of the paper, sustaining it through disastrous floods and devastating wars. Throughout World War II, news hungry Elmirans who couldn't wait for the daily publication to hit the streets gathered at a Market Street window where, at 11 a.m., a bulletin board was displayed with the latest war headlines and casualty lists.

The same dedication prevailed through the ruinous 1946 and 1972 floods, when chocolate-colored waters swamped the city, including the *Star-Gazette* plant, causing

evacuation of half the city's 46,000 population. In the paper's tradition, it continued publication, never missing a day, using the *Ithaca Journal* plant.

Moving smoothly through the computer and electronic age, the newspaper has its own web site for news and advertising and has received messages from as far away as Saipan in the western Pacific from Elmira natives keeping track of their hometown. While the paper's history is important, its focus is on the future and adapting to the needs of the community, says Publisher Margaret E. Buchanan.

With all the progress, the core element remains the same, Buchanan said.

"It's still people gathering information and putting it together in ways that will help them understand what's happening and how it relates to the rest of the world," Buchanan said.

Frank E. Gannett, Founder, Gannett Company.

Frank Tripp, Publisher, 1922-1964.

Time Warner Cable

When Chemung County residents received their first Cable Television Signal in 1956, few were aware that it was one of the first areas in the country to have the service. The service now offered by Time Warner Cable originally was provided by Connolly Electric Co. back in the early '50s, just shortly after the onset of broadcast television nationally.

others that provide all forms of art, information, and entertainment, as well as financial and educational programming.

Time Warner also is continuing on a course that promises intriguing advances in the future. With the development in the fiber-optics industry, the company can only hint at what is to come. Time Warner is "developing digital systems with fiber-optic applications

very bright. That means that we'll have a lot to offer in the way of information, entertainment, and communications," the Time Warner spokesman said.

Subscribers are benefiting with a system that has brought the community closer by allowing residents to keep in touch with friends, family, and business issues, but most importantly, with "pure information," and it is continually improving.

Time Warner technology has a positive effect on the economy of the area. This technology encourages businesses to locate in the area.

Time Warner's goal is to listen to customers' needs and to provide the highest quality service. The future is really . . . unlimited! ❧

Time Warner Cable, Horseheads, New York.

The Chemung County cable television system was one of the first in the nation. The hilly topography made it difficult to receive signals with the conventional metal antennae that spiked the homes of nearly everyone with a TV set. "Most homes were only able to receive two or three channels before cable television was introduced to this area," a spokesman for Time Warner Cable said.

As a pioneer in an exciting new medium, the area's first cable system provided six channels from its Elmira office. Today, Time Warner Cable offers over 80 channels to its more than 26,000 subscribers. These channels include Cable News Network (CNN), C-SPAN, the Weather Channel, and many

that will offer even more exciting opportunities," such as digital satellite music channels, home security services, and telephone services—all within the next five years.

From its first system, the local cable service has advanced to ownership by a global concern with cutting edge technology that has brought local residents to the forefront of developing services. For example, Time Warner Cable's High Speed Internet Access service, called "Road Runner," was tested in Elmira for two years before it was available nationally.

"So by having the largest multimedia organization in the world as the parent company, the future for area subscribers is

Imaging and Sensing Technology

When Westinghouse Electric Company announced its intentions in 1988 to sell a large part of its Horseheads, N.Y., operation, four of the company's senior managers put their combined experiences and wallets on the table when they decided to buy a segment of the Westinghouse business and start their own company.

It was considered such a brash and daring move that a Westinghouse planner working on the buyout dubbed the men the "Gang of Four" when discussing them in company memos. The name—embodying the risky nature of the venture—stuck temporarily. Within months, it was clear that the new operation was going without a hitch, validating the faith of about 200 workers who had decided to stay with the new firm.

The partnership—Philip Ponzi, chairman and chief executive officer; Roy Kyles, president; and Lou Binetti and David Dalrymple, executive vice presidents—seemed unusual, with the four leaders sharing equal ownership and power. But they knew the products. They knew the markets. They knew the people. And they were dedicated to their employees. With mutual respect and confidence in one another, trust in their individual strengths and their shared entrepreneurial spirit, things clicked.

Today, Imaging and Sensing Technology Corporation (IST) has become a global concern, designing and manufacturing electronic systems and components for the nuclear, defense, and chemical industries. IST employs more than 450 persons in seven manufacturing facilities around the world, and has markets as far-ranging as China, Korea, England, France, and the Czech Republic.

IST's diverse product range includes sensors and controls for the monitoring of nuclear power plants, highly specialized cathode ray tubes and displays for the defense and film recording industries, radiation-tolerant and high temperature camera systems for visual inspections in hazardous environments, light sources for analytical instruments, and high current switches for chemical production and metals processing plants.

Its products hold the unique distinction of being the first camera on the moon, used in the Hubble Space Telescope and Mars Viking Orbiter, and with helping to provide the computerized images in such Hollywood film hits as *Toy Story* and *Jurassic Park*.

Military contracts now make up less than 10 percent of IST's products. Instead, the company has focused on building a more stable base by broadening its product lines and developing new technology through acquisitions and partnering. To meet the challenges of today's market, IST works closely with all of its customers. Often products are engineered and developed solely for the customers' specific needs. "This is now our strongest suit. If a customer calls with a problem, somebody grabs a suitcase and is there tomorrow," said Dave Dalrymple.

The four original owners—still equal partners—remain the same. They also have held true to their values: concern for their customers, quality, technology, community, and especially their own employees. As a result IST has become a stronger and more diverse company. Annual sales have climbed to almost $60 million, with a payroll of $15 million.

Yet while the company continues to grow globally, it maintains its local focus and concern for its employees, as it upholds its policy of open communications, integrity, and honesty.

Imaging and Sensing Technology's Officers.

"I'd like IST to continue to be a company we are all proud to be a part of . . . where people feel they really make a difference . . . and feel they have secure futures," said Phil Ponzi.

Progressive Transportation Services, Inc.

Progressive Transportation has a long and interesting history in Elmira and the Chemung Valley. The first "public transportation" opened for business on July 1, 1871. The service consisted of horse-drawn streetcars on fixed track. Over the decades, steam cars replaced the horses; then electric trolleys replaced the steam.

As many as seven separate companies operated trolleys to various locations, such as Elmira/Horseheads, West Side Railway, Maple Ave. Railway, etc. Throughout the next 60 years, the trolley companies consolidated with Elmira Water and Light Co. (later New York State Electric and Gas) as the sole operator. In 1939 buses replaced the trolleys.

Throughout the 1940s, '50s, and '60s, several private carriers operated bus service to a rapidly decreasing market. In 1971, Chemung County took the lead and established the

New Chemung County Transportation Center.

Chemung County Transit System, utilizing private carriers. In 1980, American Transit Corp. became the operator, with Tom Freeman as the system manager. In 1988, Freeman and partners Carl Berman and Joe Boardman formed Progressive Transportation and set out to become the largest private bus carrier in New York State, providing countywide bus service in 16 New York State counties.

In 1996, Progressive merged with Coach USA to become part of the largest bus company in the United States. Coach USA is a publicly traded stock company with over $1 billion in annual sales.

1939 parade, the final day of the use of electric trolley.

Anchor Glass Container Corporation

On almost any trip to the grocery store, chances are a shopper picks up a glass container manufactured at the Anchor Glass Company plant on McCann's Blvd., Elmira Heights. It may be a jar of spaghetti sauce, a container of peaches, or a bottle of beer.

Throughout the day, around the clock, the plant's 350 employees keep two 2,800-degree furnaces going, melting 600 tons of sand, soda ash, limestone, and crushed recycled glass into clear and amber molten glass. After refining, the hot ooze is channeled into six bottle-forming machines that churn out 1.5 million food and beverage containers a day— or 166,000 tons of bottles a year in some 600 shapes and sizes. Turnaround time from raw material to shipping is 12 to 18 hours.

Despite the speed, quality is the top priority. And now Anchor Glass, the site of the former Thatcher Glass Manufacturing Co., has risen in ratings from near the bottom to close to the top in quality, and at times is number one among the company's 10 plants across the country.

It wasn't always that way. In its tumultuous history, the plant shut down for six months in 1984 when Thatcher's went bankrupt before being purchased by Anchor. At another point, the high cost of electricity in the fiercely competitive industry almost closed the plant's

doors to end the glass manufacturing tradition in the Southern Tier that began when Thatcher's built the plant in 1914.

Michael Sopp, general manager since 1989, decided it wasn't going to happen. The plant had done everything possible to become a low-cost producer of a quality product: installed more efficient machines, downsized the workforce, and spent millions on energy-saving improvements.

"But power is a large part of our costs. Our sister plants in other states were paying far less; we could not remain competitive paying our high local utility rates," Sopp says.

Approaching political figures from the county legislature to state senators and assemblymen, and even the governor, Sopp resolved the problem. Anchor was allowed to purchase 90 percent of its power from the New York Power Authority, saving the plant about $370,000 a year as it runs full tilt around the clock.

"Today, we're the shining star for Anchor in terms of quality, productivity, and total customer satisfaction," Sopp says. He credits the turnaround to aggressive cost-cutting and a total-quality program that relies heavily on strong partnerships with employees and customers.

In an almost unheard-of move, the three unions honored Sopp with a plaque for saving the plant. Sopp tossed the plaudits right back to the workers.

"It takes the entire team. They're dedicated; they're loyal; they're resilient; they're survivors. Everything begins with leadership, but that isn't just myself; it's the leadership of my staff and the three unions. Without their support, it would all come apart," Sopp says.

Now the plant is in the enviable position of being "oversold." It has more orders than production capability. That means the possibility soon of substantial capital investments that will increase production, reducing overall manufacturing costs and making the plant even more competitive.

Anchor is one of the solid manufacturing companies in Chemung County, with all of its managers actively involved in local charities. Sopp also is proud of the plant's economic impact on the community. It has an annual payroll of more than $18 million, with a direct and indirect impact on the area of about $90 million.

Seneca Beverage Corp.

Seneca Beverage Corp. is a story of growth, determination, and hard work by a man who began in the business when he was five years old, sorting bottles in his father's plant in Syracuse.

The Elmira Heights distributorship, covering Chemung, Steuben, Schuyler, Cortland, and Tompkins Counties, was founded by John F. Potter on June 3, 1968. By then, Potter had worked in every phase of the business with his father, washing trucks, operating a forklift, and setting up displays. He attended Burdette School of Accounting in Boston, returned to his father's business for a year, then decided it was time to be on his own.

At 22, he was the youngest Anheuser-Busch beer wholesaler in the country when he bought the business on June 3, 1968. He began with a staff of 17, selling about 250,000 cases of beer a year. Now, having incorporated a trucking phase into the business, he employs 105, and sells over two million cases a year from his 65,000-square-foot facility at 388 Upper Oakwood Avenue. He also has a truck facility in Elmira Heights and one in Baldwinsville, N.Y.

In addition to Anheuser-Busch, Seneca Beverage distributes Coors, Heineken, Labatt, Pabst, Snapple, and Saratoga Waters through the five-county area. The trucking business ranges even further, hauling beer throughout the New England states, eastern Pennsylvania and Virginia, New Jersey, and New York.

In the beginning, Potter says it was "the bank and debt and a little bit of luck." His friends say hard work played a large part in the company's success. In the early days, he and his wife, Trudy, cleaned the offices, and he's still apt to deliver an order of beer if need be. That happened at a concert he was enjoying at Tag's in Big Flats when he discovered they were running short. Potter disappeared and soon returned with a truckload of beer.

At a 30th anniversary celebration in June 1998, Potter said, "It's our people who make us what we are." That attitude—treating workers with respect—could account for the fact that Seneca Beverage has so many long-term employees; the general manager was once a truck driver, and the head bookkeeper

started with the firm when she was 15. And the Potters' son, John, who had worked for the business part-time for 10 years, joined the company on a full-time basis in December 1997.

Potter also credits the area with the company's success, saying that it has been extremely good for his family. His "payback" has been impressive. In 1996, he earned the Distinguished Citizen Award from the Five Rivers Council of the Boy Scouts of America, served on its board, as well as the Chemung Canal Trust Co., and was chairman of Southern Tier Economic Growth and a trustee of Elmira College.

Potter continues to work hard at expanding his business, buying out distributorships in Corning, Hornell, and the Ithaca area. Planning is one of his keys to success.

"If you don't know where you're going, you can't get there," he says. ✍

Elmira Water Board

*T*he adage "necessity is the mother of invention" could apply to the development of the Elmira water system. It also took the ingenuity of pioneer families, who were determined to provide the area with the best possible water system.

And, while it started with crude wooden mains, it progressed through the years to become a model for other cities throughout the country. Two of its general managers, John M. Diven (1875-1905) and John G. Copley (1942-1972), have been credited with the foresight to make it happen. Both were recognized nationally in the water industry— each serving terms as president of the American Water Works Association.

The first hint of an organized system came in 1858, when Isaac Hobie built a wooden bulkhead across Seeley Creek in Southport and laid wood pipes to provide water to a small number of homes and businesses in the Broadway area. Two years later Civil War Gen. Alexander M. Diven and his sons, George M. and John M. Diven directed construction of the Hoffman Street dam on Hoffman Creek to provide water to the downtown area. The Divens ran the Elmira Water Co. as a privately owned system for 30 years.

The most significant development came in 1896 with a severe outbreak of typhoid fever that brought death to 46 of the 425 local cases. It was clear that improved water

Elmira Water Board, new filtration plant.

purification was needed. The next year a mechanical filtration plant was built on water company property adjacent to the distributing reservoir on Reservoir Street, west of Hoffman Street.

The plant—in operation until 1996—consisted of 24 two-story cypress vats containing rapid sand filters. It served as a model for cities across America as a "state-of-the-art" water system. Elmira Water, Light, and Railroad Company took over the system in 1900, bringing chlorination to the water supply in 1909. Elmira was one of the first cities in the country to use chlorine in its system.

Public operation of the water system began in 1915 when the new Elmira Water Board purchased the operation. There were 8,782 households served by about 100 miles of underground water mains. The Elmira Water Board now maintains more than 215 miles of water mains, which pump about 7 million gallons of water every day to 18,731 households, businesses, and government facilities in Elmira, Elmira Heights, portions of Horseheads, and Southport.

This constant expansion has required additions to the main plant and a

never-ending round of replacements to underground facilities. To increase supplies and augment water drawn from the Chemung River, the board in 50 years had built four reservoirs and added new wells. The system also has been coaxed and mended to operate for more than 100 years. Then in the early 1990s, it became clear that a new system was necessary.

A $25 million modernization program from 1993 to 1996 brought construction of a new concrete gravity dam in the Chemung River, a new dual media filtration plant, new Chemung river intakes, and a new pumping station on Winsor Ave.

The system provides the average customer with 44,880 gallons every year—or 122 gallons a day. With careful planning by the Elmira Water Board and with anticipation of changing regulations and population, the new system should be up to the task for at least another 50 years.

Elmira Water Board, old filtration plant.

Corning Incorporated

Corning Incorporated, one of the oldest industrial firms in America, has a rich tradition of research and development that has created leading-edge technologies for some of the fastest growing segments of the world's economy.

Always innovative, the Fortune 500 firm has moved from being a company once known for its housewares products, to being a global company providing technology for the information superhighway, as well as for the information display, environmental, life sciences, and advanced materials markets.

Corning traces its roots to 1851, when Amory Houghton purchased an interest in the Bay State Glass Co. in Cambridge, Mass. In 1864, the company bought the Brooklyn Flint Glass Company. Four years later, attracted by ample coal and good transportation facilities, the company was transferred to Corning, N.Y. and renamed Corning Flint Glass Company. It was incorporated in 1875 as Corning Glass Works and renamed Corning Incorporated in 1989.

The region's largest employer, Corning is a worldwide market leader in optical fiber and photonic components; television and computer display glass; and advanced materials for the scientific and environmental marketplaces. It has more than 16,000 employees and dozens of plants worldwide, including facilities in Big Flats, Corning, and Erwin, N.Y.

The company has a history of achievement in glass technology that shows a pattern of resolve in researching uncharted fields. After discussions with Thomas Edison in 1879, the company developed and produced the glass envelope needed for the inventor's incandescent lamp. As that business grew, Corning, in 1926, invented a machine to mass-produce the bulbs.

Moving into housewares products in 1915, Corning discovered a low-expansion glass and created its popular Pyrex baking dishes. Due to a shift of strategic focus toward high technology and high-growth

markets, the consumer products division was sold in 1997. Pyrex® laboratory glassware remains a part of Corning.

In 1934, the company built the 200-inch mirror for the Mt. Palomar telescope, then the world's largest piece of cast glass. In the late 1940s, Corning pioneered the mass production of black-and-white television glass, which made TV viewing affordable to millions. It came out with color-TV glass in the 1960s. In 1970, Corning scientists were the first to demonstrate the feasibility of communicating with pulses of laser light through hair-thin strands of glass fiber. Corning remains the world leader in fiber optics.

The company's innovative spirit led to its receipt, in 1994, of the National Medal of Technology given by the U.S. Department of Commerce—the nation's highest honor of its type. The Department cited the company's life-enhancing inventions, which made possible entire new industries such as lighting, television, and optical communications.

Today, Corning continues to focus on technological fields where it expects to find the most explosive growth. Corning considers its core strength to be technological leadership in specialty glass, ceramics, and photonics, as well as specialty polymers and surfaces.

With 1998 sales of $3.5 billion, Corning Incorporated's days of being a simple, mid-19th-century glass company are long past. ❧

Elmira Floral Products, Inc.

Acres of roses under glass add an aura of springtime 12 months of the year at Elmira Floral Products, Inc., East Fourteenth Street, Elmira Heights.

The company, growing roses under glass since 1903, produces more than five million blooms a year, selling wholesale to florists within a 150-mile radius of the area. And while roses are the main flower under production, lilies, alstroemeria, snapdragons, and other blooms have been added to the mix.

An off-base weather forecaster was largely responsible for the location, the concern at the turn of the century. A group of Canadian entrepreneurs were lured to the area by a unknown weatherman, who mistakingly rhapsodized that Elmira has almost 300 sunny days a year. Their business collapsed within two years, but a consortium of Elmirans took over.

With proper light, heat, and soil mix, the local growers found the key to success that had eluded the Canadians. Experimenting and expanding through the years, the company has enlarged its three acres of greenhouses to 4.75 acres and sends out—depending on the time of the year—30,000 to 50,000 blooms a week.

Company officers are President Raymond (Ron) Lowman and Vice President Peter Lowman, great-grandsons of Seymour Lowman, one of the original group of Elmira founders, who later became lieutenant governor of New York State in 1925 and Assistant Secretary Treasury in 1927.

When Seymour Lowman left for Washington, he turned the business over to his only son, A. Marshall Lowman, an engineer and contractor who owned Lowman Construction Co. The new owner ran the business, performed distinguished public service throughout the county, and became a renowned and unflappable trouble-shooter for many corporations and institutions.

After World War II, his son, Marshall (Rip) Lowman, father of the firm's current officers, graduated from Dartmouth College, attended Cornell University's School of Horticulture, joined the company, and became president in 1970.

The current owners have continued their father's policy of focusing on the quality of the product as they experiment with an array of new species. The company grows 43 varieties, or shades, but red remains the most popular since men, the major buyers, equate red roses with romance. Women, however, prefer the more imaginative corals, soft pinks, and lavenders, Ron Lowman says.

Still, "special occasion" flowers, such as white roses for weddings and funerals, are an important part of the business. The company's three refrigerated trucks deliver fresh-cut blooms five days a week to area florists.

While the company continues to experiment, expansion is limited because of the high costs of the light and heat needed to spur growth. Instead, the company is attempting to diversify, growing flowers that are difficult to ship to the United States from the South American market.

Roses remain the company's mainstay, but a variety of other blooms are finding their way into the specialty greenhouses. A rose by any other name may smell as sweet . . . but other heartier blooms are also being grown to meet regional florists' needs.

Arnot Realty Corporation

While the name Arnot Realty Corporation has become almost synonymous with the Arnot Mall in Big Flats, its projects are much more far-reaching, and its history traces back to families who were involved in the early development of the community.

The Arnot Realty Corporation and The Rathbone Corporation were founded in 1906 to manage the real estate holdings and financial investments of the three children of

Branch Canal near Athens, Pennsylvania.) and in the building of the Erie Railroad from Binghamton to Corning. He was one of the founders of the area's first bank—the Chemung Canal Trust Co.—which is still the area's largest independent commercial bank. He also owned a considerable amount of real estate throughout the area. The Arnot Ogden Medical Center and Arnot Art Museum bear perpetual testimony to the

County. His descendants are still active in community development projects. Directing Arnot Realty Corporation on a daily basis are John Brand III and Frederick Q. Falck, great, great, great grandsons of John Arnot. Other family members are still officers.

Arnot Realty's faith in the growth of the area is responsible for the development of Hickory Grove Apartments, a 200-unit complex of upscale garden apartments with a swimming pool, clubhouse, workout rooms, and a physical fitness center. The complex is geared for senior citizens, who no longer want the responsibility of home ownership, young married couples, and corporate executives, who will be working in the area for short periods of time.

"We believe the market needs it. We feel the area's economy is extremely strong and we're reacting to the need for multiple family homes," an Arnot Realty spokesman said.

Arnot Realty, being locally owned and locally managed, gears itself to the well-being of our community.

Harriet Tuttle Arnot (1859-1919) and James Bailey Rathbone (1851-1919). Mrs. Rathbone was the granddaughter of John Arnot, who immigrated to this country from Scotland in 1801 and who became a very successful banker and venturesome businessman.

Mr. Arnot was instrumental in forming the Junction Canal (which connected the Chemung Canal in Elmira with the North

name of a family, whose influence ranged from the development of Arnot, Pennsylvania for its coal resources to Arnot Forest near Sullivanville, where thousands of acres of lumber were harvested.

Three branches of the family—the Falcks, Rathbones, and Hoffmans—continued John Arnot's pursuit of development that would add to the quality of life in Chemung

Arnot Mall

*T*oday, it would be difficult to imagine Chemung County without the Arnot Mall Shopping Center. But in the early 1960s, it was an innovative venture that would require considerable imagination, hard work, and risk.

With the upswing in shopping centers nationwide, Arnot Realty felt that the Twin Tiers was ready for one—and Arnot was prepared to take it on. They wanted more than just a place to shop. They envisioned it as a community center where people throughout the area would meet to stroll, dine, go to the movies, and attend charity fairs, art exhibits, and other events, all in a controlled atmospheric environment.

And, it would add a new beat to the community. Visitors from a wide area could come to shop, as well as attend nationally-known tourist attractions already in place throughout the region.

After years of planning and construction, under the direction of now retired Arnot Realty president Ernst K. Edelmann, the Mall opened in 1967 as the largest enclosed shopping center between Rochester and New York City. It started with 37 stores, anchored by Iszard's Department Store (in the space now occupied by Bon Tons) and with J.C. Penney, which is still in its original position.

Arnot Mall provided acres of parking, together with an interior made up of fountains, trees, hanging planters, and benches for a restful and attractive environment. However, in 1980, it was time to move ahead. In a dramatic expansion, the Mall went from 370,000 square feet to the one million square feet that it is today. It has 120 stores that include not only J.C. Penney and Bon Ton as anchor stores, but Sears, Roebuck and Co., Kaufmanns and Bradlees, along with a wide range of boutiques and specialty shops.

With its many services and retail stores, Mall developers think of it as "the shopping hub of Chemung County." It draws from a

Aerial view of Arnot Mall.

50-mile radius, placing it, in the vernacular of the industry, in the "super regional mall" category, reaching into Pennsylvania and far beyond the traditional Chemung-Steuben-Schuyler shopping area.

While only a few of the original establishments remain, the mix of stores changes as retailing evolves. Arnot Realty owners feel their local roots help provide the sensitivity to the local market's needs..

"A shopping center of such size and quality as ours is a constantly evolving entity. We are continually improving and upgrading our tenant mix to better serve our customers," an Arnot Realty spokesman says.

Southern Tier Contract, Incorporated

When Daniel Aber thinks of selling office furniture, the word "desk" seldom comes to mind. Most often, it is "work station"—and a work station is an area that is designed with the health, safety, and convenience of the worker in mind.

Aber heads Southern Tier Contract, Incorporated, a full service contract furniture dealer offering space-planning, selection, and installation to businesses and institutions throughout the Twin Tiers. But selecting office furniture is no longer just a matter of color and design. The advent of computers has brought a whole range of repetitive strain injuries that can be addressed with properly designed work areas.

Ergonomics—the study of the relationship between workers and their environments—is an important facet of the business that Aber started in 1995. Aber, a native Elmiran working with a Rochester business furniture firm, decided to start a company in Elmira after two local concerns closed shop.

Locating the office at 805 Hatch St., he rented a truck, hired part-time installers, and did his own paperwork. Now there are six employees and a company truck—and business has leaped from zero to $1.2 million a year. Southern Tier Contract covers a 45-mile radius, but also serves local companies' satellite offices in Pittsburgh, Albany, Buffalo, and Suffern, New York.

Specializing in high quality furniture, Southern Tier Contract, Incorporated has more than 100 clients, including area hospitals, insurance companies, governmental offices, and school districts. ❧

Circa 1870 view of the Chemung Canal from Washington Avenue Bridge, with the Elmira Rolling Mills in the background. Courtesy of Chemung County Historical Society, Inc.

Chemung Industry Index

Bibliography

Beauchamp, William M. "Aboriginal Place Names." *Bulletin No. 108 of the New York State Museum.* Albany: New York State Education Department, May 1907.

Byrne, Thomas E. *Chemung County, 1890-1975.* Elmira: Chemung County Historical Society, Inc., 1976.

Canal Society of New York State. *Field Trip Guide, October 31, 1998: The Chemung Canal.* Syracuse, NY: Canal Society of New York State, 1998.

Chemung County Historical Society. *Our Sense of Place: Neighborhoods in Chemung County.* Elmira: Chemung County Historical Society, Inc., 1995.

Cotton, Michelle L. *A Century of Outdoor Life and Recreation in the Southern Tier, 1865-1965.* Elmira: Chemung County Historical Society, Inc., 1984.

Cotton, Michelle L. *Mark Twain's Elmira, 1870-1910.* Elmira: Chumung County Historical Society, Inc., 1985.

Ebert, Barbara E. "Historic Overview of the City of Elmira." *Reconnaissance Survey of the City of Elmira, Chemung County, New York.* Elmira: Near Westside Neighborhood Association, Inc., 1998.

Fischer, Joseph R. *A Well-Executed Failure: The Sullivan Campaign Against the Iroquois, July-September 1779.* Columbia, SC: University of South Carolina Press, 1997.

Gruver, Rebecca Brooks. *An American History*, Vol. II. Reading, MA: Addison-Wesley Publishing Co., 1981.

History Writer's Group. *Chemung County, Its History.* Elmira: Chemung County Historical Society, Inc., 1961.

Jennings, Charles Robert. "Urban Renewal as Disaster Recovery Planning: Tropical Storm Agnes in Elmira, New York." M.A. thesis, Cornell University, 1994.

Jerome, Robert D. and Herbert A. Wisbey, Jr., Eds. *Mark Twain in Elmira.* Elmira: Mark Twain Society, Inc., 1997.

Kent, Donald H. "The Myth of Etienne Brulé." *Pennsylvania History*, October 1976.

McCracken, Richard J. "Susquehannocks, Brulé and Carantouannais: A Continuing Research Problem." Unpublished paper, 1984.

Merrill, Arch. *Southern Tier, Vol. 2.* New York: American Book—Stratford Press, Inc., 1954.

Merrill, Arch. *The Underground, Freedom's Road and Other Upstate Tales.* New York: American Book—Stratford Press, Inc., 1963.

Murray, Elsie. "Carantouan: Old Spanish Hill." *Northumberland County Historical Society Proceedings and Addresses* Vol. XVI, 1948. Reissued, Athens, PA: Tioga Point Museum, 1978.

National Park Service. *Underground Railroad: Official National Park Handbook.* Washington, DC: Division of Publications, National Park Service, 1998.

Pohlman, Richard W. "Elmira, New York: Ordering the City of Objects." M.A. thesis, Cornell University, 1986.

Rasmussen, R. Kent. *Mark Twain A to Z: The Essential Reference to His Life and Writings.* New York: Facts on File, Inc., 1995.

Ritchie, William A. *The Archaeology of New York State.* Garden City, NY: Natural History Press, 1965.

Robinson, Mitchell L. "Men of Peace in a World at War: Civilian Public Service in New York State, 1941-1946." *New York History*, April 1997.

Snow, Dean R. *The Iroquois.* Cambridge, MA: Blackwell Publishers, Inc., 1994.

Sutherland, Cara A. *150: A Celebration of Chemung County's Heritage.* Elmira: Chemung County Historical Society, Inc., 1986.

Sutherland, Cara A. *A Heritage Uncovered: The Black Experience in Upstate New York, 1800-1925.* Elmira: Chemung County Historical Society, Inc., 1988.

Sutherland, Cara A. *German Heritage of the Chemung Valley.* Elmira: Chemung County Historical Society, Inc., 1987.

Towner, Ausburn. *Our County and Its People: A History of the Valley and County of Chemung.* Syracuse: D. Mason & Co., 1892.

Periodicals:

Chemung Historical Journal. Elmira: Chemung County Historical Society, 1955-1999.

[Elmira] *Star-Gazette.*

Index